CHEFS LYNN CRAWFORD AND LORA KIRK

share their favourite family-style recipes for everyday cooking and casual celebrations at home. Creating a family meal: setting the table, sharing dishes passed around the table in large bowls or platters and enjoying it with one another is cooking at its best. Cook together and eat together—it just does not get any better than that. Sitting down and enjoying a meal together is one of the greatest gifts we can give one another.

Hearth & Home features over 140 delicious and comforting recipes—from Turkey Cheddar Biscuit Pot Pie and Honey-Garlic Ribs to Buttery Mashed Potatoes and Sweet Onion Cornbread— that are all achievable for any home cook. Most of these dishes come together quickly with few ingredients and basic techniques. Inside you will find many mains, an abundance of side dishes and show-stopping desserts to create and share a meal family-style, whether it is a quick weeknight supper, a weekend get-together or a special-occasion celebration. The book includes suggestions for building a family-style meal, but feel free to create your own feast of shared plates.

Hearth & Home

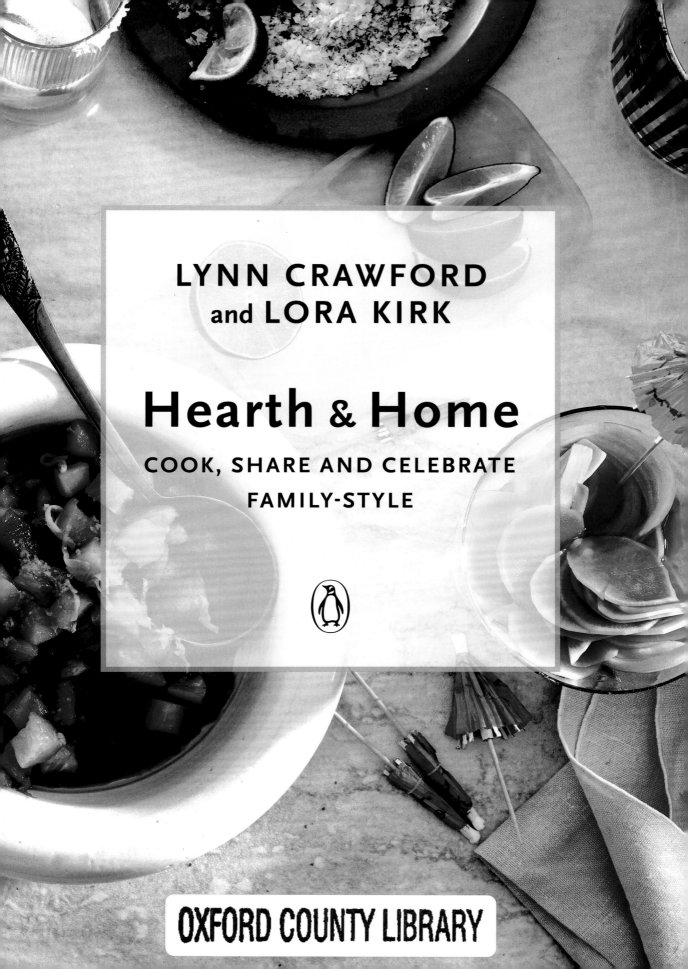

LYNN CRAWFORD and LORA KIRK

Hearth & Home

COOK, SHARE AND CELEBRATE

FAMILY-STYLE

PENGUIN

an imprint of Penguin Canada, a division of Penguin Random House Canada Limited

Canada • USA • UK • Ireland • Australia • New Zealand • India • South Africa • China

First published 2021

www.penguinrandomhouse.ca

Library and Archives Canada Cataloguing in Publication

Title: Hearth & home : cook, share and celebrate family-style / Lynn Crawford and Lora Kirk.
Other titles: Hearth and home
Names: Crawford, Lynn, author. | Kirk, Lora, author.
Identifiers: Canadiana (print) 20200406558 | Canadiana (ebook) 20200406566 | ISBN 9780735239524
    (hardcover) | ISBN 9780735239531 (EPUB)
Subjects: LCSH: Cooking. | LCGFT: Cookbooks.
Classification: LCC TX714 .C738 2021 | DDC 641.5—dc23

Cover and interior design by Terri Nimmo
Cover and interior photography by Maya Visnyei
Photo on page x by Ryan Szulc
Food and prop styling by Sasha Seymour

Printed and bound in China

10 9 8 7 6 5 4 3 2 1

Penguin
Random House
PENGUIN CANADA

FOR OUR DAUGHTERS,

Addie Pepper and Gemma Jet Aubergine,

who inspire us to cook, share the table and

see food through their eyes.

CONTENTS

SIDES

DESERTS

THE PANTRY

Spice Blends

Flavour Boosters

Stocks, Sauces, Condiments and Dressings

INTRODUCTION

The more you know about cooking, the less of a mystery it becomes. We like uncomplicated cooking. "Uncomplicated" doesn't mean it lacks creativity, flavour or integrity. It means simple, straightforward, delicious and memorable food that's not too time-consuming to make.

Home cooks that love cooking may not have the years of professional cooking experience the two of us have, but what they do have is just as much knowledge of good food and their passion for cooking it is just as strong.

We believe that good cooking has less to do with an actual recipe or technique than with the best and tastiest ingredients. Source your ingredients well. Eat locally and sustainably, and learn where your food comes from and how it is produced. Choose seasonal ingredients to inspire your meals with the most flavourful food. Support the farmers' markets in your community and learn from the producers.

Many years cooking separately and together has given our lives so much happiness and fulfillment. When we opened our market-inspired, chef-driven family-style restaurant Ruby Watchco in 2010, the only restaurants offering table d'hôte—multi-course meals at a fixed price—were fine-dining restaurants and hotels. We were far from either. Unlike most restaurants, we served only four courses a night. Basically, you didn't choose your meal—we told you what you were having. And—unorthodox for the time—we educated our diners, listing on our menu the provenance of our ingredients. Like farm-to-table chefs and restaurateurs Jonathan Waxman and Alice Waters before us, we saw the power in passed, shared plates of made-from-scratch fare, and the feeling of community and camaraderie it fostered.

However, it was not easy. Going out for a four-course meal was seen as a weekend thing back then, and eating a big meal still requires planning on the guests' part. No large or late lunch; they have to save room (we are known for our large portions). Luckily, our four-course meals made with local, seasonal and sustainable ingredients caught on, and a decade later we have garnered critical acclaim as one of the best restaurants in Toronto and Canada.

Things have changed so much since then. Here in Toronto, there are now dozens of restaurants that serve only tasting menus. And these days, it's de rigueur for everyone from coffee shops to fine-dining establishments to list on the menu the farms and producers their ingredients came from.

—

Working separately in London and New York and then opening our own restaurants in Toronto, we've learned how to make complex, intricate dishes for hundreds of people. But when we're at home, we opt for "uncomplicated" stocking our fridge, freezer and pantry with both staples and flavour-boosters—aromatics, pastes, oils and sauces that magnify and enhance dishes.

We take our inspiration from everywhere—dining out, magazines, cookbooks, walks through farmers' markets and food shops—and constantly experiment with flavour pairings. We lean into our cravings a lot. If we feel like vegetarian, no doubt you will find us grabbing our homemade curry powder and chopping up veg for Potato Aloo Chaat with Tamarind Chutney, Cilantro Yogurt and Bhel Puri (page 177). And we often hanker for our favourite takeout dishes. Even after a long day working, we'll still fire up the stove, because General Gemma's Chicken (page 50), however late, makes everything better.

Whether we're cooking for just us or for a large crowd, at the cottage or in the heart of the city, that feeling of hearth and home is constant—that feeling of creating a meal for friends and family whatever the size, of setting the table, sharing dishes and celebrating coming together. It just does not get any better than that.

Food tells the story of your family—past, present and even what you aspire to be. Whether you're cooking a quick stir-fry, a slow roast or a multi-component dish, memories are created with each recipe and every meal.

We are thrilled to share our recipes with you in this book. Despite being professional chefs, we promise we have made them achievable for any home cook. Most of these dishes come together quickly with few ingredients and basic techniques. You do not have to have seven different knives or a counter full of specialized appliances. In these pages you will find many mains and an abundance of side dishes to create and share a meal family-style, whether it is a quick weeknight supper, a weekend get-together or a special-occasion celebration. We offer "Eat with" suggestions for building a family-style meal, but feel free to create your own feast of shared plates to enjoy.

We want to inspire you to cook—and to cook together with your family and friends. Get everyone involved, especially children. When children have the experience of cooking, they learn the value and pleasure of good food.

Cook together and eat together. Sitting down and enjoying a meal together is one of the greatest gifts we can give one another.

Good food comes from good ingredients and your passion for cooking. We hope this collection of recipes will help you put many exciting, enticing meals on the table that everyone will enjoy. And we guarantee they'll make it into your regular rotation.

From our family to yours,
Lynn and Lora

VEGETARIAN

Sweet Potato and Lentil Coconut Thai Curry

This fragrant Thai-style stew hits all the right notes with aromatic fresh ginger, garlic, cumin and a homemade red curry paste. The coconut milk mellows and loosens the potato and lentil mixture just enough so that it can be spooned over rice. We make this curry dish often at our home—a big pot of it for dinner and leftovers for lunches.

Making truly authentic Thai curry pastes requires serious effort and expertise. We both love Thai food so much that we wanted to create a homemade paste that we could whip up quickly and that would give us the freshest and most fragrant curry ever. Of course, if you are short on time, you can use 2 tablespoons of store-bought Thai red curry paste instead.

Feel free to change up the vegetables. Just remember to cut them all fairly small and about the same size. Try broccoli, cauliflower, mushrooms, diced butternut squash or sliced zucchini.

MAKE THE RED CURRY PASTE

1. Place the chilies in a medium bowl, cover with boiling water and set aside to soften, about 15 minutes. Drain the chilies.
2. Heat a small skillet over medium-high heat. Add the cumin, coriander and paprika and cook, stirring together, until fragrant, about 1 minute. Remove from the heat.
3. In a food processor, combine the chilies, garlic, shallots, ginger, lemongrass and 2 tablespoons of the olive oil and process until smooth. Add the toasted spices, cilantro, shrimp paste and lime zest and juice and continue to process until smooth. Use immediately, or spoon the curry paste into a jar, cover with a thin layer of the remaining 1 tablespoon olive oil, cover with a lid and store in the refrigerator for up to 2 weeks.

MAKE THE CURRY

4. Heat the olive oil in a large pot over medium-high heat. Add the onion and cook, stirring frequently, until softened, 3 to 4 minutes. Add the turmeric, cumin, ginger, garlic and 2 tablespoons of the red curry paste. Cook, stirring, until fragrant, 1 to 2 minutes. Add the coconut milk and tomatoes and bring to a boil. Add the sweet potatoes and lentils, then season to taste with salt and pepper. Cover and cook for 45 minutes or until the sweet potatoes are soft. Remove from the heat and stir in the cilantro and lemon zest and juice. Ladle into a large serving dish and garnish with more cilantro.

EAT WITH
Tempura Broccolini with Curry Leaf Mayonnaise (page 190)

SERVES 4

Red Curry Paste
12 dried Kashmiri chilies
2 teaspoons ground cumin
1 teaspoon ground coriander
1 teaspoon smoked paprika
3 cloves garlic, chopped
2 shallots, chopped
1 tablespoon chopped peeled fresh ginger
1 stalk lemongrass (white part only), chopped
3 tablespoons olive oil, divided
¼ cup fresh cilantro leaves
2 teaspoons shrimp paste
Zest and juice of 1 lime

Curry
2 tablespoons olive oil
1 white onion, finely diced
1 tablespoon ground turmeric
1 tablespoon ground cumin
1 tablespoon minced peeled fresh ginger
1 tablespoon minced garlic
2 cans (14 ounces/400 mL each) full-fat coconut milk
2 cans (14 ounces/398 mL each) diced tomatoes
2 large sweet potatoes, peeled and cubed
1 can (14 ounces/398 mL) lentils, drained and rinsed
Kosher salt and freshly ground black pepper
½ cup fresh cilantro leaves, chopped, more for garnish
Zest and juice of ½ lemon

For serving
Steamed jasmine rice or couscous

Carrot Vindaloo with Raita and Green Chutney

This fiery Goan curry is traditionally made with chicken, but our love of local carrots made this version a no-brainer. Brimming with carrots, onion and tomatoes in fragrant, warm Indian spices, Kashmiri chili and ginger, this carrot-centric stew is phenomenal. Raita is an incredibly versatile cooling yogurt sauce that is always welcome alongside spicy foods.

You can swap in any hearty root vegetable, such as parsnips, celery root or rutabaga. For added crunch, serve with thin, crisp pappadums.

MAKE THE RAITA

1. Place the ingredients in a small bowl and stir together. Use immediately or store in an airtight container in the refrigerator for up to 1 week.

MAKE THE CARROT VINDALOO

2. Preheat the oven to 375°F.
3. Heat 2 tablespoons of the olive oil in a large skillet over medium heat. Add the carrots, season with salt and pepper, and roast in the skillet, turning frequently, until golden, about 10 minutes. Transfer the carrots to a deep casserole dish.
4. In the same skillet, over medium heat, melt the butter with the remaining 1 tablespoon olive oil. Add the onion and cook, stirring occasionally, until softened, about 10 minutes. Stir in the honey, ginger and garlic and cook until caramelized, about 2 minutes. Add the chilies, curry powder and cloves and cook, stirring, until fragrant, about 1 minute. Add the white wine vinegar and cook until the white wine vinegar has reduced by half, about 2 minutes. Add the diced tomatoes, stir together well and season with salt and pepper. Bring the sauce to a boil, then pour over the carrots. Cover with foil and bake until the carrots are tender, 25 to 30 minutes. Sprinkle with the dill and serve with bowls of raita and green chutney.

EAT WITH
Basmati Rice with Spiced Tomato Chutney (page 141)
+
Hoisin-Glazed Eggplant with Sesame Miso Baba Ganoush (page 170)

SERVES 4 TO 6

Raita
1 cup plain full-fat Greek yogurt
½ cup seeded and diced English or Persian cucumber
2 tablespoons chopped fresh dill
1 tablespoon lemon juice
1 teaspoon Garam Masala (page 228 or store-bought)
½ teaspoon ground cumin
Kosher salt and freshly ground black pepper to taste

Carrot Vindaloo
3 tablespoons olive oil, divided
2 bunches of carrots with tops, trimmed and peeled
Kosher salt and freshly ground black pepper
2 tablespoons unsalted butter
1 cup finely diced yellow onion
2 tablespoons honey
1 tablespoon grated peeled fresh ginger
1 tablespoon minced garlic
1 to 2 dried Kashmiri chilies (or ½ teaspoon red chili flakes)
2 tablespoons curry powder
⅛ teaspoon ground cloves
¼ cup white wine vinegar
1 can (28 ounces/796 mL) diced tomatoes
¼ cup chopped fresh dill, for garnish

Green Chutney (page 242), for serving

Eggplant Parmigiana

Baked eggplant Parmesan is a delicious vegetarian dinner. This recipe simplifies the classic Italian dish for a quick prep, so it's extremely easy to make and a fun project for two people in the kitchen. This one is perfect for feeding a group of your favourite people or sharing between two and having leftovers all week. Serve it on its own, over a bed of pasta or with some garlicky sautéed greens.

MAKE THE MARINARA SAUCE

1. Pour the tomatoes into a large bowl and crush with your hands. Pour the water into the can and swirl to get all the tomato juices; set aside.
2. Heat the olive oil in a large skillet over medium heat. When the oil is hot, add the garlic. Stir the garlic with a wooden spoon for 1 minute, until golden, then add the tomatoes, reserved tomato water, salt, sugar and chili flakes. Stir together.
3. Add the basil sprigs, including stems, and simmer until the sauce has thickened and the oil on the surface is a deep orange, about 15 minutes. Remove the basil and discard. Keep the sauce warm until ready to serve.

PREPARE THE EGGPLANT

4. Position a rack 2 or 3 inches under the broiler. Set the oven to broil.
5. Place the flour, eggs and breadcrumbs in 3 separate shallow dishes. Season the eggplant with salt and pepper. Working with one slice of eggplant at a time, dredge the eggplant in the flour, then dip into the egg, letting the excess drip off, then coat in the breadcrumbs. Transfer to a plate.
6. Heat 2 tablespoons of the olive oil in a large skillet over medium-high heat. Working in batches, and adding the remaining olive oil as needed, cook the eggplant, flipping once, until golden on each side, 2 to 3 minutes per side.
7. Transfer the cooked eggplant to a baking sheet in a single layer. Spoon the marinara sauce over each eggplant round, then top each with a slice of provolone cheese. Place the eggplant under the broiler and cook until the cheese is golden and bubbly, 3 to 4 minutes. Serve garnished with Parmesan, basil pesto and basil leaves.

EAT WITH
Cannellini Bean, Kale and Tomato Ragout (page 158)
+
Polenta with Butternut Squash, Swiss Chard and Mascarpone (page 174)

SERVES 4 TO 6

Marinara Sauce
1 can (28 ounces/796 mL) whole San Marzano tomatoes
1 cup water
¼ cup extra-virgin olive oil
6 cloves garlic, thinly sliced
1 teaspoon kosher salt
1 teaspoon granulated sugar
Pinch of red chili flakes
2 large sprigs fresh basil

Eggplant
½ cup all-purpose flour
3 large eggs, beaten
1½ cups dry breadcrumbs
2 medium globe eggplants, sliced into eight ½-inch rounds
Kosher salt and freshly ground black pepper
½ cup olive oil, divided
8 slices provolone cheese

For serving
¾ cup grated Parmesan cheese
Basil Pesto (page 36)
Fresh basil leaves

Korean Barbecue Tofu Lettuce Wraps

We cannot get enough of Korean cuisine. Bi bim bap, bulgogi, scallion pancakes, kimchi—we want it all! Visits to Koreatown do not happen as often as we'd like these days, so we satisfy our cravings for those rich, sweet, salty, sour, tangy, spicy flavours by recreating our favourite dishes at home. This sticky, sweet deep-fried tofu is remarkably quick and easy to make and delivers a deep umami richness that is so satisfying and indulgent. It takes plain old tofu to the next level, and makes a great base for colourful Korean bowls.

Use firm, extra-firm or super-firm tofu, which are made with less water and when cubed will hold their shape.

MAKE THE NAPA CABBAGE KIMCHI SLAW

1. In a large bowl, toss together the cabbage, carrot, cilantro, lime zest and juice, kimchi, olive oil and sesame oil. Season with salt and pepper. The slaw can be stored, covered, in the refrigerator for up to 2 days.

MAKE THE KOREAN BARBECUE SAUCE

2. In a medium bowl, stir together the ingredients.

COOK THE TOFU

3. Dice the tofu into 1-inch cubes. In a large bowl, combine the tofu, cornstarch and salt. Toss to coat the tofu.
4. Heat enough canola oil to cover the bottom of a large nonstick skillet over medium-high heat. When the oil is hot, add the tofu, in two batches if necessary. Do not overcrowd the pan. Brown the tofu on all sides until crispy, 2 to 3 minutes, per side. Transfer the cooked tofu to a medium bowl. Wipe the pan clean.
5. In the same pan, over low heat, heat the Korean barbecue sauce for 1 minute. Add the tofu to the sauce. Toss to coat the tofu and cook for a minute or so.
6. Transfer to a serving platter or bowl and sprinkle with the sesame seeds and green onions. Serve the tofu on top of the napa cabbage kimchi slaw in lettuce cups.

EAT WITH
Roasted Oyster Mushrooms with Miso Garlic Butter
and Miso Brittle (page 181)
+
Zucchini Parmesan Fritters with Hot Chili Honey (page 194)

SERVES 4 TO 6

Napa Cabbage Kimchi Slaw

4 cups thinly sliced napa cabbage
1 cup grated peeled carrots
¼ cup fresh cilantro leaves, roughly chopped
Zest and juice of 1 lime
⅓ cup Kimchi (page 244 or store-bought)
2 tablespoons olive oil
1 teaspoon sesame oil
Kosher salt and freshly ground black pepper

Korean Barbecue Sauce

2 tablespoons brown sugar
2 tablespoons gochujang paste
1 tablespoon apple cider vinegar
2 teaspoons grated peeled fresh ginger
2 teaspoons grated garlic
1 teaspoon ground turmeric
1 teaspoon sesame oil
½ teaspoon black pepper

Tofu

1 block (1 pound/450 g) extra-firm tofu
½ cup cornstarch
1 teaspoon kosher salt
Canola or vegetable oil, for frying

For serving

Toasted sesame seeds
2 green onions, thinly sliced
1 head iceberg lettuce, separated into leaf cups, for serving

Portobello Mushroom Steaks with Creamed Spinach and Red Wine Shallot Sauce

Back when we lived in New York, we would go to Peter Luger Steak House for a juicy steak thickly crusted with freshly crushed peppercorns. Nowadays we eat less red meat, but we wanted to recreate the steakhouse flavours we love with a fabulous meaty vegetable.

For this French-inspired mushroom steak, use the biggest portobello mushrooms (full-grown cremini mushrooms) you can find. This filet mignon of the mushroom world, thanks to its meaty texture and earthy flavour, gets seasoned well with a steak marinade before being roasted, and is served with creamed spinach and a red wine shallot sauce.

MAKE THE PORTOBELLO MUSHROOM STEAKS WITH CREAMED SPINACH

1. Preheat the oven to 400°F.
2. In a medium bowl, toss the mushroom caps with the steak and everything marinade and let stand for 20 to 30 minutes.
3. Coat a 13 x 9-inch baking dish with the olive oil. Lay the mushrooms gill side up in a single layer in the baking dish. Spoon any remaining marinade into each mushroom cap. Bake, uncovered, until tender, about 15 minutes. Keep warm.
4. Melt the butter in a large skillet over medium heat. Add the shallot and garlic and cook, stirring, until softened, 2 to 3 minutes. Add the cream and cook until reduced by half. Whisk in the goat cheese and spinach. Continue to cook until the spinach wilts and the sauce thickens, about 3 minutes. Stir in the Parmesan and season with salt and pepper. Remove from the heat and keep warm.

MAKE THE RED WINE SHALLOT SAUCE

5. In a small saucepan, bring the shallots and red wine to a boil and cook until the wine is reduced by half and slightly syrupy, about 5 minutes. Remove from the heat. Whisk in the butter, one piece at a time, to make a glossy sauce. Season to taste with salt and pepper.
6. To serve, arrange the mushroom caps on a serving platter. Evenly divide the creamed spinach over the mushrooms. Sprinkle with the crispy panko breadcrumbs. Serve the stuffed mushrooms with the red wine shallot sauce on the side.

EAT WITH
Castelfranco Radicchio, Orange and Burrata Salad with Walnut Date Vinaigrette (page 118)
+
Sweet Onion Cornbread (page 150)

SERVES 4 TO 6

Portobello Mushroom Steaks with Creamed Spinach
4 to 6 large portobello mushrooms, stems discarded
¼ cup Steak and Everything Marinade (page 234)
2 tablespoons olive oil
1 tablespoon unsalted butter
1 shallot, finely diced
1 teaspoon minced garlic
½ cup heavy (35%) cream
2 tablespoons soft goat cheese
6 cups packed baby spinach
3 tablespoons grated Parmesan cheese
Kosher salt and freshly ground black pepper
3 tablespoons Crispy Panko Breadcrumbs (page 232)

Red Wine Shallot Sauce
2 tablespoons finely diced shallots
1 cup red wine
6 tablespoons chilled unsalted butter, cubed
Kosher salt and freshly ground black pepper

Butternut Squash with Thanksgiving Trimmings

You do not have to wait for the holidays to enjoy the flavours of the season. This celebratory recipe brings together all the joyful bounty of Thanksgiving dinner in one stunning dish. The beautiful maple-roasted Hasselback squash takes centre stage, with lots of support from the nutty toasted walnuts and tart cranberries.

The Hasselback—thin, close-together slices that stop just short of the base—does not just make the dish look extraordinary. It allows for all those flavours and tidbits to sink into the squash, delivering tasty morsels with every bite.

ROAST THE BUTTERNUT SQUASH

1. Preheat the oven to 425°F. Line a baking sheet with parchment paper.
2. Using a peeler, remove the skin and the white flesh from the squash. Cut the squash in half lengthwise. Scoop out and discard the seeds. Rub the olive oil all over the squash, then season with salt and pepper. Place the squash halves cut side down on the prepared baking sheet and roast until the squash begins to soften, about 15 minutes.

MEANWHILE, MAKE THE GLAZE

3. In a small saucepan, combine the ingredients. Cook over medium heat, stirring, until the sugar dissolves, 3 to 4 minutes. Remove from the heat.

CONTINUE ROASTING THE BUTTERNUT SQUASH

4. Remove the squash from the oven and transfer to a cutting board. Using a sharp knife, slice rounded sides of the squash halves crosswise, ¼ inch thick, going as deep as possible but without cutting all the way through. Return the squash to the baking sheet, scored sides up. Spoon half of the glaze over the squash, allowing it to drip into the cuts. Season with salt and pepper.
5. Roast the squash for 30 minutes, then spoon the remaining glaze over the squash. Roast until the squash is tender, 15 to 20 minutes.

MEANWHILE, MAKE THE THANKSGIVING TRIMMINGS

6. While the squash continues to roast, melt the butter in a large skillet over medium-high heat. Stir in the shallots and cook, stirring frequently, until softened, 2 to 3 minutes. Add the Brussels sprout leaves, cranberries and walnuts. Toss together and cook, stirring, until the leaves turn bright green and are just wilted, about 2 minutes. Remove from the heat and stir in the sage and parsley, then season with salt and pepper.
7. Transfer the squash to a serving platter. Drizzle over any glaze left on the pan. Top with the Thanksgiving trimmings.

EAT WITH
Leek and Spinach Pie (page 193)
+
Roasted Oyster Mushrooms with Miso Garlic Butter and
Miso Brittle (page 181)

SERVES 6 TO 8

Butternut Squash
1 large butternut squash
2 tablespoons extra-virgin olive oil
Kosher salt and freshly ground black pepper

Glaze
¼ cup lightly packed brown sugar
1 tablespoon maple syrup
1 tablespoon unsalted butter
½ teaspoon Harissa Paste (page 233 or store-bought)
¼ teaspoon cinnamon
¼ teaspoon nutmeg

Thanksgiving Trimmings
2 tablespoons unsalted butter
2 shallots, minced
2 cups Brussels sprout leaves
½ cup dried cranberries
½ cup toasted walnuts, roughly chopped
4 fresh sage leaves, chopped
2 tablespoons chopped fresh flat-leaf parsley
Kosher salt and freshly ground black pepper

Spaghetti Squash Pad Thai

Spaghetti squash is insanely fun to eat, no matter your age. Scraping the flesh to create long noodle-like threads is like raking a little garden, but way more satisfying and delicious. Not only is spaghetti squash a fun food, it is loaded with potassium, vitamins C and A and other antioxidants. Adding to the appeal, it is low in calories—about forty calories in one cup cooked—as well as fat, sodium and carbohydrates. This tasty alternative to pasta is also high in fibre to keep you feeling full longer.

Instead of topping the squash with a typical tomato sauce, the sweet, sour, tangy flavours of pad Thai—predominantly from tamarind—heighten this dish in a new and unexpected way. Capping it off with crisp bean sprouts, peanuts and cilantro makes it as delectable as the restaurant version we love so much.

MAKE THE PAD THAI SAUCE

1. Heat the canola oil in a medium saucepan over medium heat. Add the shallots and cook, stirring occasionally, until tender, 2 to 3 minutes. Add the pineapple, ginger and honey and cook, stirring occasionally, until caramelized, about 5 minutes. Transfer the mixture to a blender.
2. Add the tamarind date paste, soy sauce, Sriracha sauce and fish sauce and blend until will mixed. Strain the sauce through a fine-mesh sieve into a small bowl and set aside.

COOK THE SPAGHETTI SQUASH AND TOFU

3. Preheat the oven to 425°F. Line 2 baking sheets with parchment paper.
4. Carefully cut the spaghetti squash in half lengthwise and scoop out and discard the seeds. Place the squash cut side up on a prepared baking sheet. Season with salt and pepper, cover with foil and roast until tender, 35 to 40 minutes.
5. Meanwhile, spread the tofu on the second prepared baking sheet. Drizzle with 2 tablespoons of the canola oil and season with salt and pepper. Roast until golden brown, about 15 minutes.
6. Heat a large skillet over high heat. Add the remaining 1 tablespoon canola oil, shallots and garlic and cook, stirring frequently, until softened, about 3 minutes. Add the carrots, bell pepper and baked tofu. Cook until the vegetables are tender, another 2 to 3 minutes. Add the spinach and green onions and cook until the spinach begins to wilt, 1 to 2 minutes. Pour 2 tablespoons of the pad Thai sauce into the pan and toss to coat.
7. Using a fork, carefully scoop the squash out of the skin, reserving the shells. Add half of the squash noodles to the pan, toss, and cook for 1 minute. Stir in the remaining noodles and pad Thai sauce. Add the bean sprouts and toss together.
8. To serve, spoon the squash filling into the squash shells and arrange on a serving platter. Garnish with peanuts, cilantro and lime wedges.

SERVES 4 TO 6

Pad Thai Sauce

2 tablespoons canola oil
2 tablespoons finely diced shallots
½ cup diced pineapple
2 tablespoons finely diced peeled fresh ginger
2 tablespoons honey
3 tablespoons Tamarind Date Paste (page 234)
2 tablespoons soy sauce
2 teaspoons Sriracha sauce
1 teaspoon fish sauce

Spaghetti Squash and Tofu

1 spaghetti squash
Kosher salt and freshly ground black pepper
1 package (12 ounces/350 g) extra-firm tofu, drained and diced
3 tablespoons canola oil, divided
4 shallots, thinly sliced
3 large cloves garlic, minced
2 carrots, peeled and cut into matchsticks
1 red bell pepper, thinly sliced
2 cups packed baby spinach
4 green onions, thinly sliced on the diagonal
1 cup bean sprouts

Garnishes

Chopped unsalted peanuts
Fresh cilantro leaves
Lime wedges

EAT WITH
Gai Lan with Chili Jam (page 166)
+
Hoisin-Glazed Eggplant with Sesame Miso Baba Ganoush (page 170)

Chilies Rellenos with Tomato Cilantro Salsa and Tomatillo Salsa

Stuffed peppers can be so boring, but these Mexican roasted poblano peppers stuffed with black beans and whipped goat cheese are anything but basic. Shallow-frying and then baking results in a crispy exterior surrounding a pillowy-soft cheesy filling that we think is more scrumptious than one overflowing with meat.

For a dairy-free option, swap out the goat cheese for herb tofu ricotta.

PREPARE THE POBLANO PEPPERS

1. Place the poblanos directly on a gas burner, under a hot broiler or on a hot charcoal or gas grill and char, turning a few times with tongs, until blackened all over, 8 to 10 minutes. Transfer to a large bowl, cover with plastic wrap and let steam for 15 minutes.

2. Place the blackened poblanos on a work surface. Gently rub the peppers with a paper towel to remove the skins, taking care not to tear the flesh. Using a paring knife, cut a slit lengthwise from the stem to halfway down each pepper. Remove and discard the seeds.

MAKE THE FILLING AND STUFF THE POBLANOS

3. Heat the olive oil in a large skillet over medium-high heat. Add the red onion and garlic and cook, stirring often, until soft, 4 to 5 minutes. Stir in the cumin and black beans and continue cooking until fragrant, 2 to 3 minutes. Transfer the bean mixture to a large bowl.

4. Stir the cream cheese and goat cheese into the bean mixture until smooth. Stir in the cilantro, then season with salt and pepper.

5. To stuff the peppers, divide the filling into 6 equal portions. Hold a poblano open with one hand and stuff with a portion of the mixture with the other hand. Do not overstuff.

MAKE THE TOMATO CILANTRO SALSA

6. Position a rack 6 inches under the broiler. Set the oven to broil.

7. Arrange the plum tomatoes on one third of a baking sheet. Place the onion, garlic and jalapeños on the middle third of the baking sheet and the tomatillos on the last third. Place the baking sheet under the broiler to soften and slightly blacken everything, 10 to 15 minutes.

8. Transfer the tomatoes, half of the onions, half of the garlic and 1 jalapeño to a high-speed blender. Add the tomato purée and chili powder. Purée until smooth, then season with salt and pepper. Transfer the salsa to a medium bowl and rinse out the blender.

MAKE THE TOMATILLO SALSA

9. Place the tomatillos and the remaining onions, garlic and jalapeño in the blender. Add the cilantro and lime juice. Purée until smooth, then season with salt and pepper. Transfer the salsa to a medium bowl.

Recipe continues . . .

SERVES 6

Chilies Rellenos
6 poblano peppers
2 tablespoons olive oil
½ white onion, finely diced
2 cloves garlic, minced
1 teaspoon ground cumin
1 cup canned black beans, drained and rinsed
½ cup cream cheese, at room temperature
¼ cup soft goat cheese
¼ cup packed fresh cilantro, chopped
Kosher salt and freshly ground black pepper
4 large eggs, separated
1 cup all-purpose flour, divided
3 to 4 cups vegetable oil, for deep-frying

Tomato Cilantro Salsa and Tomatillo Salsa
1 pound (450 g) plum tomatoes, cut in half lengthwise
1 red onion, cut into 6 wedges
4 cloves garlic, peeled
2 jalapeño peppers, stems and seeds removed
1 pound (450 g) tomatillos, husked and cut in half
1 cup tomato purée
2 teaspoons chili powder
Kosher salt and freshly ground black pepper
½ cup packed fresh cilantro, roughly chopped
2 tablespoons lime juice

For serving
4 ounces (115 g) Oaxaca or ricotta cheese, cut into bite-size pieces
Fresh cilantro

Recipe continued from previous page . . .

MAKE THE BATTER AND DEEP-FRY THE STUFFED POBLANOS

10. In a medium bowl, whisk the egg whites to stiff peaks. In another medium bowl, whisk the egg yolks with ½ cup of the flour and 1 teaspoon salt until thickened slightly and pale. Whisk half of the egg whites into the yolk mixture until smooth. Gently fold in the remaining egg whites.

11. In a large cast-iron skillet, heat the vegetable oil over medium-high heat to 375°F. Line a rimmed baking sheet with a wire rack.

12. Transfer the remaining ½ cup flour to a shallow dish. Dredge 3 poblanos, one at a time, in the flour, turning to evenly coat. Gently tap off excess flour, then dip the peppers, one at a time, into the egg batter to fully submerge, allowing any excess batter to fall back into the bowl. Carefully lower the peppers, one at a time, into the hot oil. Fry, turning once halfway through, until puffed and golden brown, 5 to 7 minutes. Transfer with a slotted spoon to the wire rack. Repeat with the remaining 3 poblanos.

13. To serve, spread the tomato cilantro salsa on one side of a serving platter and spread the tomatillo salsa on the other side. Top with the fried poblanos, Oaxaca cheese and cilantro.

EAT WITH
Creamy Spinach Parmesan Orzo (page 165)
+
Honey Mustard Carrot Slaw (page 133)
+/or
Apple and Fennel Cabbage Slaw (page 133)

NOODLES

Butternut Squash Carbonara with Tempeh Bacon and Aged Gouda

Pasta carbonara is a classic, but we decided to make the indulgent dish vegetarian, using one of our favourite vegetables—butternut squash—and smoky tempeh in place of the bacon. However, we cannot live without a sumptuous cheese to go with it. A robust classic Dutch aged Gouda gives that zesty bite that enhances the dish.

You can sub in any squash, root vegetable or spiralized vegetables such as zucchini.

1. Heat 1 tablespoon of the olive oil with the butter in a large saucepan over medium-high heat. Add the onion and cook, stirring frequently, until softened, 3 to 4 minutes. Stir in the garlic and chili flakes and cook, stirring constantly, for 30 seconds. Add the butternut squash, vegetable stock and thyme leaves, and season with salt and pepper. Bring to a boil, then reduce the heat and simmer until the squash is tender, about 20 minutes.

2. Using a handheld blender, purée the squash mixture until smooth. Add the mascarpone and blend again. Remove from the heat and cover to keep warm.

3. Heat the remaining 2 tablespoons olive oil in a medium skillet over medium heat. Add the tempeh and sage leaves and cook for 1 minute. Remove the sage leaves when crisp and set aside. Add the paprika, soy sauce and ketchup to the tempeh and cook, stirring frequently, until the tempeh is brown and crispy, 2 to 3 minutes. Remove from the heat and keep warm.

4. In a large pot of boiling salted water, cook the squash noodles, stirring occasionally, until just tender, 3 to 4 minutes. Drain the squash noodles, add them to the tempeh and gently toss together. Transfer the noodle mixture to a serving platter. Pour the squash sauce over the noodles and sprinkle with the cheese and the crispy sage leaves.

EAT WITH
Gai Lan with Chili Jam (page 166)

SERVES 4 TO 6

3 tablespoons olive oil, divided
1 tablespoon unsalted butter
1 small white onion, chopped
2 cloves garlic, minced
½ teaspoon red chili flakes
3 cups peeled and diced butternut squash
2 cups Vegetable Stock (page 238 or store-bought)
2 sprigs fresh thyme, leaves only
Kosher salt and freshly ground black pepper
¼ cup mascarpone cheese (or ½ cup heavy/35% cream)
6 ounces (170 g) tempeh, cut into ½-inch cubes
1 sprig fresh sage, leaves only
1 teaspoon smoked paprika
1 tablespoon soy sauce
1 tablespoon ketchup
6 cups spiralized butternut squash noodles (about 1¼ pounds/565 g)
½ cup grated aged Gouda or Parmesan cheese

Singapore Noodles

This dish is bursting with golden-tinted fried rice vermicelli noodles, juicy shrimp, tender-succulent chicken, Chinese barbecued pork and the star ingredient that gives that distinct flavour—curry powder. These are our all-time favourite take-out noodles, packed with so many different, intensely flavourful ingredients, and they always satisfy when that Chinese takeout craving hits. But they're so easy to make at home, and we think even more enjoyable. Fire up your wok!

You can buy char siu (prepared Chinese barbecued pork) in Chinese markets. If you cannot find it, you can substitute smoked bacon.

1. Bring a medium pot of water to a boil over medium-high heat. Add 2 tablespoons of the curry powder and 1 tablespoon of kosher salt. Add the rice vermicelli noodles and cook until just softened, about 2 minutes. Drain immediately and set aside.
2. Heat 2 tablespoons of the vegetable oil in a large wok or nonstick skillet over medium-high heat. Add the chicken and sauté for 1 minute, then add the shrimp and continue to sauté until both the chicken and shrimp are just cooked through, about 2 minutes more. Transfer the chicken and shrimp to a large bowl.
3. In the same wok, heat the remaining 2 tablespoons vegetable oil. Add the red onion and cook, stirring frequently, until browned, 2 to 3 minutes. Add the bell peppers and continue to cook for about 2 minutes. Add the cooked noodles, sprinkle with the remaining 3 tablespoons curry powder and toss together. Season with salt and pepper. Cook the noodles for 2 minutes, until fragrant. Push the noodle mixture to one side of the wok and pour the eggs into the empty side. Let the egg sit until cooked, about 1 minute, and then toss it with the noodles, breaking the egg into smaller pieces. Add the chicken, shrimp, pork, bean sprouts, green onions and soy sauce and toss well.
4. Serve in a large bowl or on a platter, garnished with shredded lettuce, crispy fried shallots and lime wedges for squeezing over the noodles.

EAT WITH
Hoisin-Glazed Eggplant with Sesame Miso Baba Ganoush (page 170)

SERVES 4 TO 6

5 tablespoons Madras curry powder, divided
Kosher salt
8 ounces (225 g) dried rice vermicelli noodles
4 tablespoons vegetable oil, divided
4 ounces (115 g) boneless, skinless chicken breast, cut into ½-inch dice
4 ounces (115 g) large shrimp (size 21–25), peeled, deveined and cut into ½-inch dice
½ cup thinly sliced red onion
1 cup thinly sliced bell peppers (mixture of red, yellow and orange)
Freshly ground black pepper
2 large eggs, beaten
4 ounces (115 g) char siu (prepared Chinese barbecued pork), cut into ½-inch dice
½ cup bean sprouts
2 green onions, thinly sliced on the diagonal
3 tablespoons soy sauce
1 cup shredded iceberg lettuce
2 tablespoons Crispy Fried Shallots (page 232)
1 lime, quartered

Dan Dan Noodles

Dan dan mian, which means "pole-carrying noodles," originate from Sichuan, China, and the name refers to the shoulder poles that noodle sellers used to carry their wares. This is our spicy variation: noodles blanketed in peanut sauce, tossed with ground pork studded with ginger and garlic, with leafy greens and a flourish of roasted peanuts at the end. Note that our chili oil condiment is very, very spicy, so you might want to add it gradually and taste as you go.

MAKE THE PEANUT SAUCE

1. Heat the canola oil in a medium saucepan over medium heat. Add the ginger, shallot, lemongrass and chili and cook, stirring constantly, for 2 minutes.
2. Add the coconut milk, peanut butter, lime zest and juice, soy sauce and sambal oelek and whisk to combine. Cook until the sauce is thoroughly heated. Remove from the heat.

MAKE THE DAN DAN NOODLES

3. Heat a large skillet over medium-high heat. Add the canola oil and ground pork and cook, stirring frequently, until the pork is browned, 3 to 4 minutes. Add the ginger, garlic, five-spice powder and chili oil. Stir together and continue cooking, stirring frequently, until the pork is fully cooked, 2 to 3 minutes. Add the hoisin sauce, dark soy sauce and Shaoxing wine and cook until the liquid has almost evaporated, about 5 minutes. Remove from the heat and keep warm.
4. Bring a large pot of salted water to a boil over high heat. When the water is boiling, add the bok choy and cook for 1 minute. Using tongs, remove the bok choy from the boiling water, drain well and add to the pork mixture.
5. Cook the egg noodles in the boiling water until soft, about 2 minutes. Reserve ½ cup of noodle water. Drain the noodles and return them to the pot. Add the peanut sauce and stir to coat the noodles, adding some of the noodle water if too thick. Transfer the noodles to a large serving bowl, top with the pork mixture and garnish with green onions and peanuts.

EAT WITH
Blistered Beans with Ginger, Black Garlic and Cashews (page 154)

SERVES 4 TO 6

Peanut Sauce

1 tablespoon canola oil
2 tablespoons minced peeled fresh ginger
1 tablespoon minced shallot
1 tablespoon minced lemongrass (white part only)
1 tablespoon minced Fresno chili
1 can (14 ounces/400 mL) full-fat coconut milk
½ cup smooth peanut butter
Zest and juice of 1 lime
2 tablespoons soy sauce
1 tablespoon sambal oelek

Dan Dan Noodles

2 tablespoons canola oil
8 ounces (225 g) ground pork
1 tablespoon finely chopped peeled fresh ginger
2 teaspoons finely chopped garlic
1 teaspoon Five-Spice Powder (page 228 or store-bought)
1 to 2 tablespoons Chili Oil (page 231), or to taste
2 tablespoons Hoisin Sauce (page 239 or store-bought)
1 tablespoon dark soy sauce
2 teaspoons Shaoxing wine or mirin
4 to 6 baby bok choy, cut lengthwise into quarters
1 pound (450 g) fresh egg noodles

Garnishes

⅓ cup finely chopped green onions
¼ cup unsalted roasted peanuts, chopped

Mushroom Bolognese with Pappardelle

Mushrooms are hidden gems in the cooking world. They are ridiculously aromatic, providing a flavour profile that no other vegetable can match. With their unique texture they are like awesome little edible sponges, absorbing the flavours of whatever they are cooked with. This Bolognese sauce is slow-cooked with lots of button mushrooms, so you will immediately taste the flavour explosion of every one of them.

We recommend buying loose rather than prepackaged mushrooms so you can inspect their condition and quality. Look for mushrooms with whole, intact caps and avoid those with discoloration or dry, shrivelled patches. The mushrooms should feel faintly damp but never moist or slimy, and their texture should be springy and light rather than spongy. Aroma is another important indicator of quality and intensity—the stronger the sweet, earthy scent, the more potent and flavourful the mushrooms.

1. In a large pot over medium-high heat, melt the butter with the olive oil. Add the onion, celery and carrot and cook, stirring occasionally, until the vegetables are softened, 6 to 8 minutes. Add the garlic and mushrooms and continue cooking until the mushrooms are browned and the vegetables are completely cooked through, 4 to 5 minutes.
2. Add the tomato paste, chili flakes and thyme and cook, stirring, until the tomato paste breaks down, about 2 minutes. Add the tomatoes, tomato juice and mushroom powder and stir to combine. Continue cooking until the sauce comes to a simmer, then reduce the heat to medium-low. Cook, stirring occasionally, until the sauce thickens, about 20 minutes. Remove and discard the thyme sprigs. Season with salt and pepper.
3. Meanwhile, bring a large pot of salted water to a boil. When the water is boiling, add the pasta and cook until al dente, 8 to 10 minutes. Drain the pasta, add to the sauce and toss. Transfer to a serving platter and sprinkle the Parmesan on top. Serve immediately.

EAT WITH
Warm Lentil Mirepoix Salad with Goat Cheese and Almonds (page 125)

SERVES 4 TO 6

2 tablespoons unsalted butter
1 tablespoon olive oil
½ cup finely diced white onion
½ cup finely diced celery
1 carrot, peeled and finely diced (about 1 cup)
4 cloves garlic, minced
1 pound (450 g) button mushrooms, sliced (about 4 cups)
1 tablespoon tomato paste
½ teaspoon red chili flakes
2 sprigs fresh thyme
1 can (28 ounces/796 mL) diced tomatoes
1 cup tomato juice
2 tablespoons Mushroom Powder (page 235)
Kosher salt and freshly ground black pepper
1 pound (450 g) dried pappardelle pasta
½ cup grated Parmesan cheese

Addie's Firecracker Noodles

It does not matter how many times we make this dish, we are like kids gazing in wonder when the noodles puff up in the hot oil. Slightly spicy, crispy, crunchy and crazy, these noodles have lots of fresh Thai flavours and are always a big favourite at parties.

In Thai, this dish is called *ee krob*, and the ingredients vary according to what is in season and on hand. We have found it works well with stir-fried shrimp, pork or chicken, so feel free to improvise.

MAKE THE THAI DRESSING

1. Combine the ingredients in a large bowl and stir together until the sugar has dissolved.

MAKE THE FIRECRACKER NOODLES

2. Cut the noodles into 4-inch lengths with scissors.
3. Line a plate with paper towel. Heat the canola oil in a medium pot over medium heat. When the oil is hot, deep-fry the noodles, a handful at a time. As soon as the noodles puff up—a matter of seconds—use a slotted spoon to transfer them to the paper towel to drain.
4. Pour off all but 2 tablespoons of the oil from the pot. Add the chili, garlic, ginger and lemongrass and cook, stirring frequently, until fragrant, about 2 minutes. Add the turkey and cook, stirring frequently, until cooked through, 4 to 5 minutes. Add about one-third of the Thai dressing and cook for another 2 to 3 minutes, until the mixture slightly thickens.
5. Scrape the turkey mixture into the bowl with the remaining Thai dressing. Toss well.
6. In a separate large bowl, combine the red onion, tomato, bean sprouts, cucumber, lettuce, basil and cilantro. Toss well.
7. Place the crispy noodles on a large serving plate and top with the turkey and vegetables.

EAT WITH
Roasted Oyster Mushrooms with Miso Garlic Butter
and Miso Brittle (page 181)

SERVES 4 TO 6

Thai Dressing
⅓ cup lime juice
3 tablespoons fish sauce
1 tablespoon brown sugar
1 teaspoon sambal oelek

Firecracker Noodles
6 ounces (170 g) dried rice vermicelli noodles
1 cup canola or peanut oil, for frying
1 Fresno chili, finely chopped
2 cloves garlic, minced
1 tablespoon finely chopped peeled fresh ginger
1 tablespoon finely chopped lemongrass (white part only)
1½ pounds (675 g) ground turkey, chicken or pork
1 small red onion, thinly sliced
1 large tomato, diced
1 cup bean sprouts
1 cup thinly sliced English cucumber
1 cup shredded iceberg lettuce
½ cup packed fresh Thai basil leaves
½ cup packed fresh cilantro leaves

Garganelli Pasta with Basil Pesto and Lemon Ricotta

You do not need to spend hours in the kitchen to cook a dish that tastes like you did! This simple recipe for pesto is made with fresh basil, olive oil and pine nuts. It's tossed with pasta and crowned with a generous finishing of ricotta, Parmesan and lemon to brighten all its vibrant flavours.

Adding a teaspoon of pesto to a dish can give it life. We always have a jar on hand to use as a sauce on pasta, a condiment in a sandwich, or to add to a soup, dressing or scrambled eggs.

MAKE THE BASIL PESTO AND COOK THE PASTA

1. Bring a large pot of salted water to a boil. Have ready a bowl of cold water. When the water is boiling, add the spinach and blanch until vibrant green, 5 seconds. Using a slotted spoon, transfer the spinach to the cold water. (Keep the water at a boil.) When the spinach is cooled, drain it and squeeze out the excess water.
2. Add the pasta to the boiling water and cook until al dente, 8 to 10 minutes.
3. While the pasta is cooking, in a food processor, combine the cooked spinach, basil and pine nuts. Pulse until coarsely chopped. Add the olive oil and Pecorino Romano and process until a smooth pesto forms. Season with salt and pepper, then transfer to a large bowl.

MAKE THE LEMON RICOTTA

4. Combine the ingredients in a medium bowl and stir together.

TO FINISH

5. Drain the pasta, reserving ½ cup of the cooking liquid. Add the pasta and reserved cooking liquid to the bowl of basil pesto. Toss until the pasta is evenly coated, then season with salt and pepper. Transfer the pesto pasta to a large serving bowl. Garnish with spoonfuls of the lemon ricotta, more grated Parmesan and the crispy panko breadcrumbs. Drizzle with the olive oil.

EAT WITH
Pea Shoot and Sweet Pea Sauté with Pancetta and Lemon (page 173)

SERVES 4 TO 6

1 pound (450 g) dried garganelli pasta

Basil Pesto
2 cups packed baby spinach
1 cup loosely packed fresh basil leaves
¼ cup pine nuts, toasted
⅓ cup olive oil, more for drizzling
½ cup grated Pecorino Romano cheese
Kosher salt and freshly ground black pepper

Lemon Ricotta
½ cup ricotta cheese
Zest and juice of 1 lemon
2 tablespoons grated Parmesan cheese, more for serving

Crispy Panko Breadcrumbs (page 232), for serving

Baked Rigatoni with Meatballs

Baked pasta dishes have to be one of the quintessential comfort foods, often bringing back happy memories of childhood family dinners. This favourite of ours is cheesy, saucy and gooey with classic Italian meatballs at their finest. A blend of beef and pork gives them richness, and a few aromatics and some cheese make them extra-flavourful. This dish comes together quickly, so it's ideal after a long day when you're hankering for the perfect home-cooked meal.

Often we cook a double batch of meatballs and freeze the extras to use for quick meals. Place the cooled cooked meatballs on a baking sheet and freeze until solid, then transfer to a freezer bag and store in the freezer for up to 3 months.

1. Preheat the oven to 400°F. Line a baking sheet with parchment paper.
2. In a large bowl, combine the pork, beef, onion, confit garlic, breadcrumbs, parsley, Old Bay seasoning and eggs. Mix well. Roll the mixture into tablespoon-size balls between wet palms to form 30 meatballs. Place the meatballs on the prepared baking sheet and bake until browned and fully cooked through, 12 to 15 minutes.
3. While the meatballs are baking, bring a large pot of salted water to a boil. When the water is boiling, add the rigatoni and cook until very al dente, about 7 minutes. Drain the pasta and reserve in strainer.
4. In a 13 x 9-inch baking dish, spread half of the pasta in an even layer. Arrange half of the meatballs and mozzarella evenly over the pasta. Evenly spoon half of the marinara sauce over the top. Repeat with the remaining pasta, meatballs, mozzarella and sauce. Top with spoonfuls of the ricotta and the Parmesan.
5. Cover with foil and bake for about 25 minutes. Uncover and bake for 5 more minutes.
6. Set the oven to broil. Broil until the top is lightly browned. Remove from the oven and let stand for 5 minutes. Serve garnished with basil and extra Parmesan.

EAT WITH
Romaine and Treviso Salad with Pancetta Vinaigrette
and Caesar Aioli (page 130)

SERVES 6 TO 8

1 pound (450 g) ground pork
1 pound (450 g) ground beef
¾ cup minced white onion
3 tablespoons Confit Garlic (page 233 or 1 tablespoon minced fresh garlic)
1 cup panko breadcrumbs
¼ cup chopped fresh flat-leaf parsley
2 teaspoons My Old Bay Seasoning (page 229 or store-bought)
2 large eggs, lightly beaten
1 pound (450 g) dried rigatoni
8 ounces (225 g) fresh mozzarella cheese, torn into 1-inch pieces
3 cups Marinara Sauce (page 11 or store-bought)
1 cup ricotta cheese
½ cup grated Parmesan cheese, more for garnish
¼ cup loosely packed fresh basil leaves, for garnish

Spaghettini with Fontina and Black Truffle

Coming from central Italy, black truffles are earthy and robust. They are often grated into warm butter with a touch of garlic to make a classic rich truffle tagliatelle. Our aromatic sauce is just a little more indulgent with cream and cheese, but it's super simple to make.

Discover the versatile prowess of flavourful truffle paste. This delicacy is made with both white and black truffles, and it is a great ingredient to have around to quickly add that characteristic pungent flavour to any dish. Mix it into scrambled eggs, risotto, mashed potatoes or a creamy soup or sauce, or simply spread it on crostini for a wonderful appetizer.

1. Bring a large pot of salted water to a boil. When the water is boiling, add the pasta and cook until al dente, 8 to 10 minutes.
2. Meanwhile, melt the butter in a large saucepan over medium heat. Add the shallots and cook, stirring occasionally, until tender, about 2 minutes. Add the cream and cook, stirring occasionally, until reduced by half, 5 to 7 minutes. Whisk in the cream cheese and Fontina until smooth. Remove from the heat and season with salt and pepper.
3. Drain the pasta and add to the cheese sauce. Stir in the truffle paste. Serve immediately, garnished with the Parmesan and chives.

EAT WITH
Cheesy Garlic Pull-Apart Bread (page 149)
+
Lyonnaise Salad with Brown Butter Parmesan Croutons (page 129)

SERVES 4 TO 6

14 ounces (400 g) dried spaghettini
1 tablespoon unsalted butter
2 tablespoons finely diced shallots
2½ cups heavy (35%) cream
¼ cup cream cheese, at room temperature
6 ounces (170 g) Fontina cheese, grated
Kosher salt and freshly ground black pepper
2 tablespoons black truffle paste, or to taste
2 tablespoons grated Parmesan cheese
2 tablespoons chopped fresh chives

POULTRY

Grilled Mojo Chicken

Wondering what to make tonight? There's nothing more satisfying than succulent, juicy, garlicky, citrusy grilled chicken. The zesty, bold flavours inspired by Cuba inject serious life into everyday chicken thighs, resulting in a wicked dish that will put you under a spell. Getting your meal mojo back could not be easier.

The marinade works for everything from pork to shrimp to vegetables to tofu, and if we ever have any salsa left over—which is almost never—we love it with tortilla chips.

MAKE THE HOT AND SMOKY MOJO SALSA

1. Heat 3 tablespoons of the olive oil in a small skillet over medium heat. Add the sweet onion, green onion and garlic and cook, stirring often, until soft and caramelized, 8 to 10 minutes. Add the anchovies (if using), brown sugar, paprika and cumin and stir together for 1 minute. Add the bell peppers and Cuban peppers and continue cooking until the peppers have softened, 2 to 3 minutes. Deglaze the pan with the white wine vinegar and cook until the liquid is reduced by half. Add the remaining 1 tablespoon olive oil and the tomato and cook until the tomato breaks down, 4 to 5 minutes. Remove from the heat, cool, then stir in the cilantro and season with salt and pepper. Store, covered, in the refrigerator for up to 3 days.

MARINATE THE MOJO CHICKEN

2. In a medium bowl, whisk together the orange juice, lime juice, olive oil, oregano, cilantro, garlic, jalapeños, cumin, kosher salt and paprika.
3. Add the chicken to the marinade and mix until well coated. Cover and marinate in the refrigerator for at least 2 hours or ideally overnight.

GRILL THE MOJO CHICKEN

4. Preheat the grill to medium-high heat, about 400°F.
5. Remove the chicken from the marinade and discard the marinade. Season the chicken with salt and pepper. Place the chicken on the grill and cook, turning occasionally, until cooked through, 10 to 14 minutes. Transfer the grilled chicken to a serving platter.
6. Grill the avocados, red onions, orange and limes until caramelized, turning the red onions and avocados halfway through cooking, 3 to 5 minutes total. Garnish the chicken with the grilled avocados, red onions and limes. Squeeze the juice from the grilled orange all over the platter. Season with sea salt. Serve with the hot and smoky mojo salsa on the side.

EAT WITH

Potato Aloo Chaat with Tamarind Chutney, Cilantro Yogurt and Bhel Puri (page 177)

+

Tempura Broccolini with Curry Leaf Mayonnaise (page 190)

SERVES 4 TO 6

Hot and Smoky Mojo Salsa (makes about 2 cups)

4 tablespoons olive oil, divided
½ small sweet onion, thinly sliced
1 green onion, thinly sliced
2 cloves garlic, minced
4 oil-packed anchovy fillets, finely chopped (optional)
1 tablespoon brown sugar
1 teaspoon smoked paprika
¼ teaspoon ground cumin
2 red bell peppers, thinly sliced lengthwise
2 Cuban peppers, seeded and thinly sliced
¼ cup white wine or sherry vinegar
1 plum tomato, grated on a box grater
¼ cup chopped fresh cilantro
Kosher salt and freshly ground black pepper

Mojo Chicken

½ cup orange juice
¼ cup lime juice
¼ cup olive oil
½ cup loosely packed fresh oregano leaves, coarsely chopped
½ cup packed fresh cilantro leaves and stems, chopped
4 cloves garlic, finely chopped
2 jalapeño peppers, seeded and sliced into rounds
2 teaspoons ground cumin
2 teaspoons kosher salt, more for seasoning
1 tablespoon smoked paprika
2 pounds (900 g) bone-in, skin-on chicken thighs and drumsticks
Freshly ground black pepper
2 avocados, unpeeled, pitted and quartered
2 red onions, sliced into ¼-inch-thick rounds
1 orange, cut in half
2 limes, cut in half
Sea salt

Five-Spice Duck Breast with Red Wine Cherry Pan Sauce

Pan-seared duck, with its crackly, crispy golden brown skin that gives way to juicy, unctuous meat, is such a treat. If it's on the menu, we are ordering it. However, some people think it is hard to replicate at home, so we created this five-spice version that is so easy to make. Really, cooking duck is no more difficult than cooking a steak.

Salting the skin before the cooking helps to draw out moisture, which results in crispy skin as the fat renders out. Duck has a layer of fat under the skin that melts flavour into the meat as it cooks, so always start cooking it skin side down. That way, the excess fat can render against the hot pan, and when you turn the meat, the skinless side will sear in its own flavourful fat.

1. With a sharp paring knife, score the skin and fat of each duck breast in a crosshatch pattern, making sure not to cut into the meat.
2. In a small bowl, stir together the five-spice powder, salt and pepper. Rub both sides of the duck breasts with the spice mixture.
3. Heat a large cast-iron skillet over high heat. Place the duck breasts in the pan skin-side down. Reduce the heat to medium and cook until the skin is very crisp and brown and the fat has rendered from under the skin, 5 to 6 minutes. Tip out any excess fat and save for another use. Turn the breasts over and cook for another 5 minutes or until medium-rare to medium doneness, still pink at the centre, or until an instant-read thermometer reads 135°F to 140°F. Transfer the duck breasts to a cutting board and let rest for 3 to 5 minutes.
4. To the same pan, over medium-high heat, add the red wine and cook, stirring to scrape up any browned bits from the bottom of the pan, until reduced to a syrup-like consistency. Stir in the chicken stock, hoisin sauce, soy sauce and honey and reduce until the sauce has thickened, about 10 minutes. Add the cherries and bring the sauce to a boil. Remove from the heat and whisk in the butter until melted. Season with salt and pepper.
5. Slice the duck breasts on the diagonal, transfer to a serving platter and spoon the sauce over the slices.

EAT WITH
Sake and Miso Braised Shallots (page 182)
+
Spätzle with Bacon and Gruyère (page 186)
+
Warm Lentil Mirepoix Salad with Goat Cheese
and Almonds (page 125)

SERVES 4 TO 6

4 boneless, skin-on duck breasts (6 to 8 ounces/170 to 225 g each)
2 tablespoons Five-Spice Powder (page 228 or store-bought)
2 teaspoons kosher salt, more for seasoning
1 teaspoon freshly ground black pepper, more for seasoning
¼ cup dry red wine
¾ cup Roasted Chicken Stock (page 237 or store-bought)
2 tablespoons Hoisin Sauce (page 239 or store-bought)
1 tablespoon soy sauce
1 tablespoon honey
½ cup fresh or frozen pitted sweet cherries
2 tablespoons cold unsalted butter

Turkey Cheddar Biscuit Pot Pie

Pot pie is the ultimate cozy comfort food. In this recipe, tender poached cubes of turkey nestle in a rich, thick cream sauce decked out with carrots, potatoes and onions, all topped with our famous cheddar cheese biscuits. The biscuits are perfect on their own and will become an everyday family favourite in your home, too.

MAKE THE CHEDDAR CHEESE BISCUIT DOUGH

1. In a food processor, combine the flour, sugar, baking powder, pepper, baking soda and salt. Pulse to blend. Add the butter and pulse until a fine meal forms. Transfer the mixture to a large bowl. Stir in the cheese. Cover and chill in the refrigerator for at least 20 minutes. The dough can be prepared to this point up to 4 hours ahead.

2. Mix up to 1 cup of buttermilk into the dough to bind it. Turn the dough out onto a floured surface and knead gently until combined, about 10 turns. Using a rolling pin, roll out the dough to ¾-inch thickness. Using a 3-inch cookie cutter, cut out biscuits. Reroll the dough scraps and cut additional biscuits. You should have at least 12 biscuits. (To bake biscuits on their own, preheat the oven to 400°F. Arrange the biscuits on an ungreased baking sheet. Brush with the egg wash. Bake until golden brown and firm to touch, about 18 minutes. Serve warm.)

MAKE THE TURKEY POT PIE

3. Preheat the oven to 375°F.

4. Heat the olive oil in a large skillet over medium-high heat. Add the turkey and season well with salt and pepper. Cook, stirring occasionally, until the turkey is lightly browned on all sides, 4 to 5 minutes total. (The turkey will not be cooked through.) Transfer the turkey to a large bowl.

5. Return the skillet to medium heat and add 2 tablespoons of the butter, the onion, carrots and celery and cook, stirring occasionally, until the onions have softened, about 5 minutes. Add the vegetables to the bowl of turkey.

6. In the same skillet, over medium heat, combine the remaining ½ cup butter and the flour. Stir together until mixed well. Slowly whisk in the chicken stock, making sure you whisk well to avoid lumps. Bring to a boil, then add the cream, potatoes, thyme and rosemary. Add the turkey and cooked vegetable mixture and any juices from the bowl. Season with salt and pepper and simmer, stirring occasionally, until the potatoes and turkey are cooked, 8 to 10 minutes. Remove the thyme and rosemary. sprigs. Gently ladle the filling into a large casserole dish.

7. Evenly top the filling with 12 biscuit dough rounds. (You will have extra biscuits that can be baked separately.) Brush the biscuits with the beaten egg and bake until the biscuits are golden and the gravy mixture is bubbling, about 20 minutes. Cool slightly before serving.

EAT WITH
Buttery Mashed Potatoes (page 134)
+
Romaine and Treviso Salad with Pancetta Vinaigrette
and Caesar Aioli (page 130)

SERVES 6 TO 8

Cheddar Cheese Biscuits (makes at least 12 biscuits)

2 cups all-purpose flour
1 tablespoon granulated sugar
2½ teaspoons baking powder
1 teaspoon black pepper
½ teaspoon baking soda
½ teaspoon kosher salt
6 tablespoons cold unsalted butter, cut into ½-inch pieces
1¼ cups grated extra-sharp cheddar cheese
1 cup cold buttermilk, or as needed
1 egg, beaten

Turkey Pot Pie

2 tablespoons olive oil
12 ounces (340 g) boneless, skinless turkey breast, cut into 1-inch cubes
Kosher salt and freshly ground black pepper
2 tablespoons + ½ cup unsalted butter, at room temperature, divided
1 cup diced white onion
1 cup diced peeled carrots
1 cup diced celery
½ cup all-purpose flour
3 cups Roasted Chicken Stock (page 237 or store-bought)
½ cup heavy (35%) cream
1 cup peeled and diced Yukon Gold potato
1 sprig fresh thyme
1 sprig fresh rosemary

General Gemma's Chicken

Despite her young age, our daughter Gemma knows what she wants, and quite often it is chicken. Chinese takeout at our house always includes General Tao's chicken, and despite the kick of heat, our two girls love it, so we decided to make our own version.

In this recipe, diced chicken is coated in a ravishing sauce that is slightly sweet and gets a kick of heat from chilies. It's tossed together with whatever veggies we have on hand and served with noodles or rice. A quick meal that comes together easily but still feels like a treat.

1. In a medium bowl, combine the chicken, ⅓ cup of the cornstarch, 2 tablespoons of the soy sauce and the egg. Toss well to coat the chicken, then set aside to marinate for 15 minutes.

2. In a small bowl, combine the chicken stock, honey, tomato paste, rice wine vinegar and the remaining 1 tablespoon cornstarch and ¼ cup soy sauce. Whisk to combine. Set aside.

3. Line a baking sheet with paper towel. In a large, deep skillet, heat 3 inches of canola oil to 375°F over medium-high heat. Working in batches, use your hands or a slotted spoon to lift the chicken from the marinade, shake off any excess and carefully add to the oil. Cook, stirring occasionally, until the chicken is crispy and cooked through, 4 to 5 minutes. Using a slotted spoon, transfer the chicken to the paper towel to drain.

4. Heat 2 tablespoons of the canola oil in a large skillet over medium-high heat. Add the ginger, garlic and chili flakes and cook, stirring, for 1 minute, until fragrant. Stir in the chicken stock mixture and bring to a boil, then adjust the heat to maintain a strong simmer. Cook, stirring occasionally, until the sauce is thickened and glossy, 3 to 4 minutes. Add the cooked chicken and stir well to coat with the sauce. Continue cooking until the chicken is heated through, about 2 minutes more. Transfer the chicken to a serving platter and enjoy immediately.

EAT WITH
Basmati Rice with Spiced Tomato Chutney (page 141)
+
Blistered Beans with Ginger, Black Garlic and Cashews (page 154)

SERVES 4 TO 6

1½ pounds (675 g) boneless, skinless chicken thighs, cut into 2-inch pieces
⅓ cup + 1 tablespoon cornstarch, divided
2 tablespoons + ¼ cup soy sauce, divided
1 large egg, lightly beaten
½ cup Roasted Chicken Stock (page 237 or store-bought)
2 tablespoons honey
1 tablespoon tomato paste
1 teaspoon rice wine vinegar
2 tablespoons canola or peanut oil, more for deep-frying
1 teaspoon minced peeled fresh ginger
1 teaspoon minced garlic
¼ teaspoon red chili flakes

Tandoori Chicken Naan Pizza

Isn't menu planning about cravings? You wake up one morning and suddenly cannot stop thinking about Indian food for dinner. Then pizza enters the scene, and now you are torn. This pizza will take care of having to make a choice!

On a family trip to Prague, we discovered an incredible outdoor food market. One of the vendors served a delectable Indian-inspired pizza with a thick, chewy crust topped with fresh ingredients. Back home, we brought two of our favourite foods together in one handheld meal: tandoori-spiced chicken with a mint cucumber salad and raita atop fluffy naan bread.

We often cook a double batch of the naan and freeze the extras. For a quick naan, pop them in your toaster straight from the freezer.

MAKE THE NAAN BREAD

1. In a large bowl, stir together the flour, sugar, baking powder, baking soda and salt. Make a well in the centre and add the yogurt, canola oil and milk. Stir everything together to form a ball. Knead for 5 minutes, on a lightly floured surface, until the dough is smooth. Cover with a kitchen towel and let sit in a warm place for 2 hours.

2. When ready to cook the naan, heat a large, heavy skillet over medium-high heat. Divide the dough into 6 balls. On a lightly floured surface, roll each ball into an oval about ¼ inch thick. Working in batches, place the naans into the hot pan and cook, turning once, until golden brown, 2 minutes per side. Transfer to a plate, brush with the melted butter and sprinkle with the sea salt. Cover with a kitchen towel to keep warm until ready to serve.

MAKE THE MINT CUCUMBER SALAD

3. In a large bowl, mix together the ingredients. Toss the salad well and season with salt and pepper. Store, covered, in the refrigerator until ready to serve.

MAKE THE BOONDI RAITA

4. In a large bowl, whisk together the yogurt, cucumber, cilantro, lemon juice and garam masala until smooth. Season with salt and pepper. Fold in the boondi just before serving.

MAKE THE TANDOORI CHICKEN

5. In a food processor, combine the red onion, garlic, ginger, yogurt, lime juice, garam masala, turmeric, and salt and pepper to taste. Pulse until smooth.

6. Transfer the yogurt mixture to a large bowl and mix in the chicken until thoroughly coated. Cover and marinate the chicken in the refrigerator for 1 hour.

7. Preheat the oven to 425°F. Line a baking sheet with foil and coat lightly with cooking spray or oil.

8. Remove the chicken from the marinade and arrange on the baking sheet. Discard the marinade. Bake until thoroughly cooked, about 20 minutes. Then broil 6 inches under the broiler for 5 minutes or until the chicken is nicely charred. Serve the tandoori chicken in a large bowl with the naan, mint cucumber salad and boondi raita on the side.

EAT WITH
Fattoush Salad with Heirloom Tomatoes and
Za'atar Pita Crisps (page 122)

SERVES 4 TO 6

Naan Bread (makes 6 naans)
2 cups all-purpose flour
1 teaspoon granulated sugar
¾ teaspoon baking powder
¾ teaspoon baking soda
¾ teaspoon kosher salt
½ cup plain full-fat yogurt
½ teaspoon canola oil
½ cup whole milk, warm
2 tablespoons unsalted butter, melted
Sea salt

Mint Cucumber Salad
1 large English cucumber, seeded and diced
2 ripe tomatoes, diced
½ red onion, thinly sliced
¼ cup fresh mint leaves, chopped
2 tablespoons lemon juice
2 tablespoons olive oil
2 teaspoons granulated sugar
½ teaspoon kosher salt, more for seasoning
Freshly ground black pepper

Boondi Raita (makes about 2 cups)
1 cup plain full-fat Greek yogurt
½ cup English cucumber, seeded and finely diced
¼ cup loosely packed fresh cilantro leaves, chopped
1 tablespoon lemon juice
1 teaspoon Garam Masala (page 228 or store-bought)
Kosher salt and freshly ground black pepper
½ cup boondi (Indian crispy chickpea snack)

Tandoori Chicken
½ red onion, diced
2 cloves garlic, peeled
1 (1-inch) piece peeled fresh ginger
½ cup plain full-fat yogurt
2 tablespoons lime juice
1 tablespoon Garam Masala (page 228 or store-bought)
1 teaspoon ground turmeric
Kosher salt and freshly ground black pepper
1½ pounds (675 g) boneless, skinless chicken thighs, cut into ½-inch pieces

Chicken Marsala

This creamy chicken dish is a revelation. Searing the chicken until golden adds a nutty depth to both skin and meat, while the luxuriously velvety sauce studded with meaty mushrooms and a heavy dose of sweet Marsala wine adds an indulgent richness. And yet the dish is both affordable and easy to make.

Simply by swapping in different mushrooms, you can significantly change the flavour profile and depth of the dish. In addition, this sauce is just brilliant on gnocchi or pasta.

1. Preheat the oven to 350°F.
2. Season the chicken breasts well with salt and pepper. Heat the olive oil in a large ovenproof skillet over medium-high heat. Place the chicken in the pan, skin side down, and cook until golden brown and crisp, about 5 minutes. Turn the chicken over, transfer the pan to the oven and cook for 10 to 12 minutes, or until the internal temperature has reached 165°F using a meat thermometer. Transfer the chicken to a cutting board and keep warm.
3. To make the sauce, return the skillet (no need to wipe it clean) to the stovetop over medium heat. Add the butter and shallots cut side down. Cook the shallots, without moving them, until they start to caramelize, 2 to 3 minutes. Add the mushrooms and garlic and stir together. Continue to cook, stirring often, until the mushrooms have browned nicely, 3 to 4 minutes. Stir in the Marsala and cook until the liquid has almost evaporated. Add the chicken stock, cream and thyme and bring to a boil, then reduce the heat and simmer until the sauce thickens, 5 to 7 minutes. Season well with salt and pepper, then stir in the parsley and mushroom powder, if using.
4. To serve, carve each chicken breast on the diagonal into 3 or 4 slices. Arrange the sliced chicken on a serving platter and pour the sauce over the chicken.

EAT WITH
Buttery Mashed Potatoes (page 134)
+
Zucchini Parmesan Fritters with Hot Chili Honey (page 194)

SERVES 4 TO 6

4 boneless, skin-on chicken breasts
(8 ounces/225 g each)
Kosher salt and freshly ground black
pepper
2 tablespoons olive oil
3 tablespoons unsalted butter
3 or 4 shallots, peeled and cut in halves
or quarters
10 ounces (280 g) button mushrooms,
sliced (about 4 cups)
2 cloves garlic, minced
½ cup sweet Marsala wine or sweet white
wine
1½ cups Roasted Chicken Stock
(page 237 or store-bought)
½ cup heavy (35%) cream
2 sprigs fresh thyme
2 tablespoons chopped fresh flat-leaf
parsley
2 teaspoons Mushroom Powder
(page 235; optional)

Maui Fried Chicken

From the moment we set foot on Maui a few years ago, we were hooked. The fresh ocean air and gentle breezes, the warm hospitality of the locals, and of course the food—all of it blew us away. In particular, a popular Hawaiian lunch of white rice, macaroni salad and bite-size pieces of tantalizingly sweet-salty chicken tossed in sweet rice flour and deep-fried.

We return to Maui annually with our daughters, who are just as enchanted by this magical place. In between visits, we make *mochiko* chicken at home. The accompaniments change from time to time, depending on what we have on hand. We especially like this version, served with charred pineapple and Spicy Ginger Lime Mayonnaise for a bit of heat while planning our next trip.

Prep and marinate the chicken the night before. This will yield better flavour, and the chicken will be much more tender.

1. In a large bowl, whisk together the coconut milk and soy sauce. Add the chicken, mixing until coated and submerged. Cover and marinate in the refrigerator for at least 4 hours or overnight.
2. In a large bowl, stir together the mochiko, cornstarch, sesame seeds, granulated sugar, garlic powder, ginger, salt and pepper. Set aside.
3. Core and peel the pineapple, then slice it lengthwise into large chunks. Heat the butter in a large nonstick skillet over high heat. Coat the pineapple wedges with the brown sugar; then place in the hot pan. Cook, turning once and shaking the pan often, until golden brown, 8 to 10 minutes total. Transfer the pineapple to a plate.
4. Line a plate with paper towel. In a large, deep skillet, heat 2 inches of vegetable oil to 360°F over medium-high heat. Using tongs, remove the chicken from the marinade, letting excess liquid drip off, and dredge in the mochiko mixture. Working in batches, fry the chicken in the hot oil until crispy and cooked through, 7 to 8 minutes, turning halfway through cooking. Using tongs, transfer the chicken to the paper towel to drain. Sprinkle with sea salt. Discard the marinade.
5. Arrange the chicken and pineapple on a serving platter. Garnish with the green onions and serve with the spicy ginger lime mayonnaise.

EAT WITH
Bacon and Egg Iceberg Salad with Avocado Dressing (page 113)
+
Lobster Potato Salad (page 126)

SERVES 6 TO 8

1 can (14 ounces/400 mL) full-fat coconut milk
½ cup soy sauce
2 pounds (900 g) boneless, skinless chicken thighs
1 cup mochiko (sweet rice flour)
¼ cup cornstarch
2 tablespoons sesame seeds
1 tablespoon granulated sugar
2 teaspoons garlic powder
2 teaspoons ground ginger
1 teaspoon kosher salt
½ teaspoon freshly ground black pepper
1 pineapple
2 tablespoons unsalted butter
½ cup packed brown sugar
Vegetable oil, for frying
Sea salt
2 green onions, cut on the diagonal, for garnish

Spicy Ginger Lime Mayonnaise (page 242), for serving

Jerk Chicken Curry with Coconut Rice

In our family we have so many favourite Jamaican recipes, like goat curry, roti, jerk chicken, fried chicken, oxtail stew, beef patties, fried plantains and ackee fish. However, this simple jerk chicken stew, made with an authentic jerk seasoning, sweet potato and coconut, is a delicious spin on the traditional Island recipe. It is slightly spicy, slightly sweet, and perfect as well with shrimp, beef or vegetables.

MAKE THE JERK CHICKEN CURRY

1. Season the chicken generously with salt and pepper. Heat the olive oil in a large pot over medium-high heat. Working in batches if necessary, place the chicken in a single layer in the pot and cook until golden brown all over, 4 to 5 minutes per side. Transfer the chicken to a plate.

2. Add the onion and carrot to the pot and cook, stirring occasionally, until softened, 4 to 5 minutes. Add the ginger, garlic and jerk marinade seasoning and cook, stirring, for 1 minute. Return the chicken to the pot with any juices. Add the sweet and Yukon Gold potatoes, chicken stock, coconut milk and thyme. Bring to a boil, then reduce the heat and simmer, stirring occasionally, until the potatoes are fork-tender, 25 to 30 minutes.

MEANWHILE, MAKE THE COCONUT RICE

3. Rinse the rice under cold running water until the water runs clear. In a medium saucepan, combine the rice, coconut milk, water, salt and ginger. Bring to a boil over high heat. When boiling, cover, reduce the heat to low and cook until the liquid is absorbed, 15 to 20 minutes. Remove the ginger slices and discard. Fluff the rice and lime zest together with a fork.

4. To serve, remove the thyme sprigs from the jerk chicken curry and discard. Ladle the curry into a large serving bowl and garnish with the cilantro. Serve the coconut rice in a bowl alongside the curry.

EAT WITH
Honey Mustard Carrot Slaw (page 133)
+/or
Apple and Fennel Cabbage Slaw (page 133)
+
Tempura Broccolini with Curry Leaf Mayonnaise (page 190)

SERVES 4 TO 6

Jerk Chicken Curry

1 to 1½ pounds (450 to 675 g) boneless, skinless chicken thighs, cut into 2-inch pieces
Kosher salt and freshly ground black pepper
2 tablespoons olive oil
1 cup diced yellow onion
1 cup diced peeled carrot
2 tablespoons minced peeled fresh ginger
1 tablespoon minced garlic
1 tablespoon Jerk Marinade (page 234 or store-bought), more to taste
2 cups diced peeled sweet potato
2 cups diced peeled Yukon Gold potato
4 cups Roasted Chicken Stock (page 237 or store-bought)
1 can (14 ounces/400 mL) full-fat coconut milk
3 sprigs fresh thyme
Fresh cilantro leaves, for garnish

Coconut Rice

1 cup white jasmine rice
1 cup full-fat coconut milk
¾ cup water
½ teaspoon kosher salt
4 thin slices peeled fresh ginger
Zest of ½ lime

Hearth Roasted Chicken

A juicy, crispy roast chicken with vegetables is one recipe every home cook can—and should—easily master. This incredibly succulent roast chicken has a smoky flavour and sweet heat that is unmistakably barbecue, thanks to the complex aromatic hearth rub and roasted garlic butter.

For juicy roast chicken, make sure to season generously and get fat over and under its skin. Butter is best, but olive oil will do too. Gently work your fingers under the skin of the breasts to separate it from the meat and work in another layer of flavour with additional butter or olive oil.

1. Preheat the oven to 350°F.
2. In a food processor, combine ½ cup of the butter, hearth barbecue rub, maple syrup, chipotle peppers and confit garlic. Purée to form a paste.
3. Use your hand to loosen the chicken skin from each breast, being careful not to tear the skin, and stuff about half of the paste mixture into the gaps. Rub the rest of the paste mixture all over the outside of the chicken.
4. Scatter the onions and potatoes in a roasting pan. Place the chicken on top of the vegetables, breast side up, and season with salt and pepper. Roast for about 1½ hours (about 20 minutes per pound/450 g), basting occasionally with the pan juices, until the chicken has reached an internal temperature of 160°F. Remove from the oven and leave in the pan for 5 to 10 minutes to rest. Lift the chicken up, letting any juices run into the pan, and transfer the chicken and vegetables to a serving platter.
5. To make a gravy, melt the remaining 2 tablespoons butter in the pan over low heat on the stovetop. Stir in the flour and cook until light brown. While stirring, gradually pour in the chicken stock and cook, stirring, for a few minutes, until the sauce thickens slightly. Strain the gravy into a sauce boat and serve with the chicken.

EAT WITH
Asparagus with Citrus, Anchovy and Almond Butter (page 153)
+
Beet Salad with Horseradish Whipped Goat Cheese and
Pistachio Granola (page 114)
+
Crispy Smashed Potatoes with Caramelized Onion Dip (page 138)

SERVES 4 TO 6

½ cup + 2 tablespoons unsalted butter, at room temperature, divided

¼ cup Hearth Barbecue Spice Rub (page 229)

3 tablespoons maple syrup

2 tablespoons chipotle peppers in adobo sauce

2 tablespoons Confit Garlic (page 233) or (1 tablespoon minced garlic)

1 free-range chicken (3 to 4 pounds/1.4 to 1.8 kg)

2 white onions, sliced into ½-inch rounds

1 pound (450 g) fingerling potatoes, cut in half lengthwise

Kosher salt and freshly ground black pepper

2 tablespoons all-purpose flour

1 cup Roasted Chicken Stock (page 237 or store-bought)

Chorizo-Stuffed Cornish Hens with Peperonata and Salsa Verde

Cornish hens really do not get the attention they deserve. They boast juicy, tender lean meat that is very mild so you can bolster it with big, bold flavours like we have done with this spicy sausage stuffing and sweet pepper and olive sauce. Their diminutive size means they cook quickly and makes them ideal for family-style dining: everyone gets their own individual bird, which also happens to look fancy and festive!

Note that you will need a meat thermometer for determining when the stuffing is safely cooked.

MAKE THE SALSA VERDE
1. In a medium bowl, combine the ingredients and mix well. Use immediately or store in an airtight container in the refrigerator for up to 1 week.

PREPARE THE CORNISH HENS
2. Preheat the oven to 425°F. In a large bowl, stir together the paprika, garlic powder, salt and pepper. Season the Cornish hens all over with half of the dry rub. Reserve the remaining dry rub for the peperonata. Stuff each hen with 4 ounces (115 g) of chorizo and place the stuffed hens, breast side up, in a roasting pan. Rub 1½ teaspoons of the olive oil over each hen. Set aside.

MAKE THE PEPERONATA
3. Line a baking sheet with parchment paper.
4. In a large bowl, mix together the ingredients. Add the remaining spice rub and toss well. Spread the vegetables on the prepared baking sheet and roast until the peppers and onions have softened, 12 to 15 minutes. Remove from the oven. Keep the oven at 425°F to roast the Cornish hens.

ROAST THE CORNISH HENS
5. Roast the hens for 15 minutes. Reduce the heat to 350°F and continue roasting, basting occasionally with the pan juices, for another 20 to 30 minutes or until the internal temperature of the thickest part of the thigh reaches 160°F and the juices run clear. Transfer the hens to a cutting board and let rest for 10 minutes before serving.
6. While the hens rest, reheat the peperonata for 5 minutes.
7. Using a sharp carving knife, slice the Cornish hens in half. Transfer the peperonata to a serving platter. Arrange the Cornish hens on top and serve with the salsa verde on the side.

SERVES 4 TO 6

Salsa Verde (makes about 1 cup)
1 cup packed fresh flat-leaf parsley leaves, finely chopped
½ cup packed fresh basil leaves, finely chopped
½ cup finely chopped pitted green olives
2 tablespoons finely chopped gherkins
1 tablespoon drained capers, finely chopped
1 tablespoon Confit Garlic (page 233) or (1 clove garlic, chopped)
1 teaspoon Dijon mustard
2 tablespoons red wine vinegar
2 tablespoons olive oil
2 teaspoons kosher salt

Chorizo-Stuffed Cornish Hens
2 teaspoons smoked paprika
2 teaspoons garlic powder
1 teaspoon kosher salt
1 teaspoon black pepper
4 Cornish hens (1½ to 2 pounds/ 675 to 900 g each), boned
1 pound (450 g) fresh chorizo sausage, casings removed
2 tablespoons olive oil

Peperonata
⅓ cup pimento-stuffed green olives
2 ripe tomatoes, cut into quarters
2 red bell peppers, cubed
1 yellow bell pepper, cubed
2 red onions, cubed
2 tablespoons olive oil
2 sprigs fresh thyme, leaves only

EAT WITH
Harissa-Roasted Parsnips with Whipped Feta, Pistachios and Rosemary Honey (page 169)
+
Lyonnaise Salad with Brown Butter Parmesan Croutons (page 129)

FISH

Fogo Island Cod Amandine

Tony Cobb and Janice Thomson are the founders of Fogo Island Fish. They started a program that revives the traditional method of hand-lining for wild cod, using one line, one hook, and hauling up by hand, resulting in zero bycatch (other fish, which are usually discarded). This hand-lined top-quality cod is the best-tasting fish you will ever have. We are honoured to know them both and to support the hardworking and passionate fishers of Fogo Island who we have so much respect for.

The best codfish in the world comes from Newfoundland and Labrador. The fish is so much cleaner and fresher. The texture—the beautiful crispy skin and the melting flesh—is something we had never before experienced. We both agree that our fresh herb and nutty pesto is the perfect accompaniment for this fish.

Use a sharp knife to remove the skin from the fish, or ask your fishmonger to remove it for you.

MAKE THE ALMOND HERB PESTO

1. In a food processor, combine the basil, parsley, dill, mint, chives, miso, confit garlic, lemon purée, mustard, almonds and 2 tablespoons of the olive oil. Process until smooth, scraping down the sides of the bowl. With the motor running, add the remaining 2 tablespoons olive oil in a slow, steady stream until the pesto has just thickened to a paste. Season with salt and pepper. Use immediately or store in an airtight container in the refrigerator for up to 2 weeks.

MAKE THE CRISPY SKIN (IF USING)

2. Preheat the oven to 400°F. Line a baking sheet with parchment paper.
3. Using a spoon, scrape any remaining fish meat from the back of the skin so the skin will get crispy when cooked.
4. Cut the skin into desired-size pieces or bake as a whole piece and shatter after cooking. Place the skin on the prepared baking sheet. Make sure the skins do not touch each other. Brush the olive oil over the skins and sprinkle with salt. Place a sheet of parchment paper and a second baking sheet on top of the fish skin. Bake until the skin is golden brown, 12 to 15 minutes. Use a thin spatula to remove the skin from the baking sheet and transfer to a plate to cool. Keep the oven at 400°F to bake the cod.

BAKE THE COD

5. Place the cod, skinned side down, on a baking sheet lined with parchment paper. Season the fish with salt and pepper. Spread just enough almond herb pesto over the fish to cover it. Bake until the fish is just cooked, 10 to 12 minutes. The fish is cooked when it flakes easily and the flesh is white throughout.
6. Transfer the fish to a serving platter and garnish with the toasted almonds and cracked crispy skin, if using. Serve with preserved lemon slices on the side.

EAT WITH

Pea Shoot and Sweet Pea Sauté with Pancetta and Lemon (page 173)

+

Roasted Cauliflower with Ricotta Salata and Lemon Caper Rémoulade (page 178)

SERVES 4 TO 6

Almond Herb Pesto (makes 1 cup)
1 cup packed fresh basil leaves
½ cup packed fresh flat-leaf parsley leaves
½ cup packed fresh dill
¼ cup packed fresh mint leaves
1 bunch of fresh chives
2 tablespoons white miso
1 tablespoon Confit Garlic (page 233) or (1 clove garlic, chopped)
1 tablespoon Lemon Purée (page 235) or (zest and juice of ½ lemon)
1 teaspoon sweet and smoky mustard (we use Kozlik's) or Dijon mustard
½ cup toasted almonds
4 tablespoons olive oil, divided
Kosher salt and freshly ground black pepper

Cod Amandine
1 side skin-on cod (2½ pounds/1.125 kg), skin removed and reserved, pin bones removed
1 to 2 tablespoons olive oil
Kosher salt and freshly ground black pepper

For serving
¼ cup toasted sliced almonds
Crispy skin (optional)
Preserved Lemon Slices (page 242)

Halibut with 'Nduja, Cauliflower, Kale and Toasted Hazelnuts

This dish is all about balancing mild, slightly sweet halibut with the slightly bitter Tuscan kale, the heat of 'nduja sausage, the creaminess of cauliflower purée and the buttery crunch of hazelnuts all in one bite. It's a winning dish that we make for our friends and family all the time.

'Nduja (pronounced *en-DOO-ya*) is a spicy spreadable sausage that tastes like fine salami. It is a specialty of the Italian region of Calabria, where it is often spread on bread or mixed into pasta sauce. Made with different parts of the pig such as the shoulder, belly and jowl, roasted peppers and a mixture of spices including paprika, 'nduja is an incredible ingredient that you should experiment with beyond this recipe.

Make sure you are not the only customer buying fish in the store. A busy fish market is a good indication that the inventory is frequently replenished and not sitting out all day. Foster a great relationship with your fishmonger so you know where your fish comes from. Most important, make sustainable seafood choices that ensure the health of our oceans for generations to come.

SERVES 6

4 cups cauliflower florets (1 large cauliflower), divided
¼ cup water
Kosher salt and freshly ground black pepper
4 tablespoons unsalted butter, divided
2½ pounds (1.125 kg) skinless halibut fillet, cut into 6 pieces
2 tablespoons olive oil
3 ounces (85 g) 'nduja sausage, casing removed, crumbled
2 tablespoons minced shallots
1 tablespoon minced garlic
1 tablespoon Lemon Purée (page 235) or (zest and juice of ½ lemon)
Zest and juice of 1 orange
Zest and juice of 1 lemon
2 cups roughly chopped Tuscan kale, stems removed
¼ cup grated Pecorino Romano cheese
¼ cup chopped toasted blanched hazelnuts

1. Place 2 cups of the cauliflower florets, the water and ½ teaspoon salt in a medium saucepan. Cover with a lid and heat over high heat until it begins to steam. Reduce the heat to medium and continue to steam until the cauliflower is tender and the water has almost evaporated, 5 to 6 minutes.

2. Transfer the cooked cauliflower and any liquid to a high-speed blender along with 2 tablespoons of the butter. Season with salt and pepper. Process to make a silky purée, adding a little more water if needed. Keep warm until ready to serve.

3. Season the halibut with salt and pepper on both sides. Heat the olive oil in a large nonstick skillet over medium-high heat. When the oil is hot, place the fish in the pan and sear until golden brown on both sides, 4 to 5 minutes per side. Transfer the fish to a large plate, cover with foil and let rest.

4. Return the pan to medium-high heat and add the 'nduja, shallots and garlic. Cook, stirring frequently, until the sausage is cooked, 2 to 3 minutes.

5. Add the remaining 2 cups cauliflower florets and cook, stirring frequently, until tender, 3 to 4 minutes. Add the lemon purée, remaining 2 tablespoons butter, orange and lemon zest and juice and kale. Cook, folding together, until the kale has completely wilted. Toss in the pecorino and season with salt and pepper.

6. To serve, spoon the cauliflower purée onto a serving platter, arrange the halibut on top and garnish with the 'nduja-cauliflower mixture. Sprinkle with the toasted hazelnuts.

EAT WITH
Creamy Spinach Parmesan Orzo (page 165)
+
Roasted Oyster Mushrooms with Miso Garlic Butter
and Miso Brittle (page 181)

EAT WITH
Endive and Apple Salad with Marcona Almonds and
Ginger Miso Dressing (page 121)
+
Sake and Miso Braised Shallots (page 182)

Bacon Okonomiyaki Pancakes with Shrimp Tempura

Pancakes loaded with fruit, chocolate and syrup usually get all the attention, but in this recipe we put the spotlight on scrumptious Japanese savoury pancakes (pronounced *oak-ah-nah-mi-yaki*), a dish we made on *Iron Chef Canada*.

With a crisp exterior that gives way to a delicate yet crunchy interior studded with bacon, green onions and cabbage, and topped with tempura shrimp, these flapjacks are a standout, whether served at brunch, dinner or as a late-night snack.

MAKE THE TONKATSU SAUCE

1. Heat the olive oil in a small saucepan over medium heat. When the oil is hot, add the shallots, garlic and ginger and cook, stirring occasionally, until the shallot is softened, 8 to 10 minutes. Add the ketchup, soy sauce, Worcestershire sauce, mirin, brown sugar, mustard and allspice and cook, stirring often, until the mixture is reduced by a third, 6 to 8 minutes. Transfer to a blender and purée until smooth. Season with salt and pepper. Use immediately or store in an airtight container in the refrigerator for up to 1 month.

MAKE THE BACON OKONOMIYAKI PANCAKES

2. Heat a large skillet over medium-high heat. Fry the bacon until almost crisp, 3 to 4 minutes. Add the cabbage and white sliced onions, stir together well with the bacon and continue to cook until the cabbage has wilted, 4 to 5 minutes. Add the green onions, stir together and cook until just wilted. Transfer the mixture to a large bowl and allow to cool.

3. In a large bowl, whisk together the ice-cold water, soy sauce, eggs, sugar, salt and togarashi. Add the flour and baking powder and mix just until the batter is smooth. Do not stir the batter too much or the pancakes will be tough. Add the cabbage mixture and stir just until everything is evenly coated.

4. Heat 1½ teaspoons of the canola oil in a small nonstick skillet over medium heat. When the oil is hot, add one-quarter of the batter. Using a spatula, press the batter down into the hot skillet to form a circle about 6 inches in diameter and ½ inch thick. Cook the pancake until golden brown on the bottom, 3 to 4 minutes, then flip and cook until golden brown on the second side. Transfer the pancake to a plate and cover with foil to keep warm. Repeat with the remaining batter, adding more canola oil to the skillet as needed.

MAKE THE SHRIMP TEMPURA

5. In a medium bowl, whisk together the flour, cornstarch and salt, then whisk in the sparkling water until just combined. Set aside.

6. Line a plate with paper towel. In a deep medium saucepan, heat 4 inches of canola oil to 365°F over medium heat. Working in batches, dip the shrimp in the batter, let excess drip back into the bowl, then gently place in the oil and cook until golden, about 3 minutes. Transfer to the paper towel to drain and sprinkle lightly with salt.

7. To serve, drizzle the tonkatsu sauce and spicy ginger lime mayonnaise over the pancakes, top with hot shrimp tempura and sprinkle with furikake seasoning and bonito flakes, if using.

SERVES 4

Tonkatsu Sauce (makes about 1 cup)
2 tablespoons olive oil
2 shallots, finely chopped
2 cloves garlic, chopped
1 (2-inch) piece fresh ginger, peeled and chopped
1 cup ketchup
¼ cup soy sauce
3 tablespoons Worcestershire sauce
2 tablespoons mirin
2 tablespoons brown sugar
1 teaspoon Dijon mustard
Pinch of ground allspice
Kosher salt and freshly ground black pepper

Bacon Okonomiyaki Pancakes
8 slices bacon, cut into 1-inch pieces
2 cups thinly sliced cabbage
½ white onion, thinly sliced
2 green onions, thinly sliced
1 cup ice-cold water
1 tablespoon soy sauce
3 large eggs
1 teaspoon granulated sugar
1 teaspoon kosher salt
½ teaspoon togarashi
1 cup all-purpose flour
1 teaspoon baking powder
2 tablespoons canola oil, divided

Shrimp Tempura
1 cup all-purpose flour
¼ cup cornstarch
½ teaspoon kosher salt, more for seasoning
1¼ cups sparkling water (or a combination of beer and sparkling water), chilled
Canola oil, for deep-frying
1 pound (450 g) large shrimp (size 21–25), peeled and deveined

For serving
Spicy Ginger Lime Mayonnaise (page 242)
Furikake Seasoning (page 232 or store-bought)
Bonito flakes (optional)

Caribbean Spiced Red Snapper Wrapped in Banana Leaves

In 2015, we were honoured to be invited to participate at the hottest annual culinary event, Cayman Cookout, hosted by Michelin-starred chef Éric Ripert, alongside participating chefs José Andrés, Daniel Boulud, Marcus Samuelsson and Anthony Bourdain. With culinary superstars, warm Caribbean breeze and sand beneath our feet, we had the best time cooking this fish on the beach under the hot sun—it was impossible not to be inspired by our surroundings. Back at home, the bright, citrusy, tropical flavours of this dish bring back wonderful memories of time spent with friends. Make a big pitcher of rum punch, turn on the reggae music and start cooking.

You may think banana leaves are hard to find, but you can often find them in the freezer section of your grocery store. Or check around Chinatown or other Chinese, Thai or Vietnamese stores in your area. If you cannot get your hands on them, though, wrap the red snapper in foil. That works just as well.

MAKE THE MANGO SALSA

1. Combine the ingredients in a medium bowl and gently toss together. Cover and refrigerate until ready to serve.

MAKE THE MARINADE

2. Combine the ingredients in a high-speed blender or food processor and purée until smooth. Transfer to a bowl.

PREPARE AND GRILL THE RED SNAPPER

3. Prepare the grill for direct cooking over medium-high heat.
4. Bring a large pot of water to a boil. When the water is boiling, plunge the banana leaves into the water for a few seconds to soften. Using tongs, remove the banana leaves and dry well with a kitchen towel. Place a banana leaf, glossy side down, on a work surface.
5. Rinse the red snapper and pat dry. Score the fish by making three or four ¼-inch-deep slashes with a knife on each side of the fish. Rub half of the marinade all over the fish and place on the banana leaf. Spread the lemongrass, ginger, chili and lime slices over the fish.
6. Fold both wide sides of the banana leaf over the fish, and then fold both ends over the fish to create a rectangular parcel. Place this parcel on the second banana leaf and wrap the fish again. Secure with toothpicks or wrap 2 strips of foil around the parcel to keep the banana leaves tight around the fish. Enclose sides and secure each side with more toothpicks or again with a strip of foil. Grill for 12 to 15 minutes per side. The fish is cooked when the flesh easily flakes away from the bones.
7. Meanwhile, warm the remaining marinade in a small saucepan over medium heat, stirring occasionally. Transfer the fish parcel to a serving plate and unwrap or cut open the banana leaves. Spread the warmed marinade over the fish. Serve with the mango salsa on the side.

SERVES 4 TO 6

Mango Salsa (makes about 2 cups)
2 ripe mangoes, peeled, pitted and diced
1 teaspoon finely chopped fresh mint
1 teaspoon minced jalapeño pepper
2 tablespoons lime juice
1 tablespoon honey

Marinade
½ cup full-fat coconut milk
¼ cup lime juice
3 cloves garlic, chopped
3 green onions, chopped
2 large shallots, chopped
1 jalapeño pepper, seeded and chopped
1 (1-inch) piece fresh ginger, peeled and chopped
1 cup loosely packed fresh cilantro, chopped
1 tablespoon fresh thyme leaves
2 teaspoons kosher salt
1 teaspoon ground coriander
1 teaspoon ground turmeric
¼ teaspoon ground allspice
¼ teaspoon cinnamon
¼ teaspoon nutmeg

Red Snapper
2 (24-inch-long) frozen banana leaves, rinsed and wiped with paper towel
1 whole red snapper (3 to 4 pounds/1.4 to 1.8 kg), gutted, fins and gills removed, and scaled
1 stalk lemongrass (white part only), thinly sliced
1 (2-inch) piece fresh ginger, peeled and thinly sliced
1 Fresno chili, thinly sliced
1 lime, sliced

EAT WITH
Basmati Rice with Spiced Tomato Chutney (page 141)
+
Gai Lan with Chili Jam (page 166)

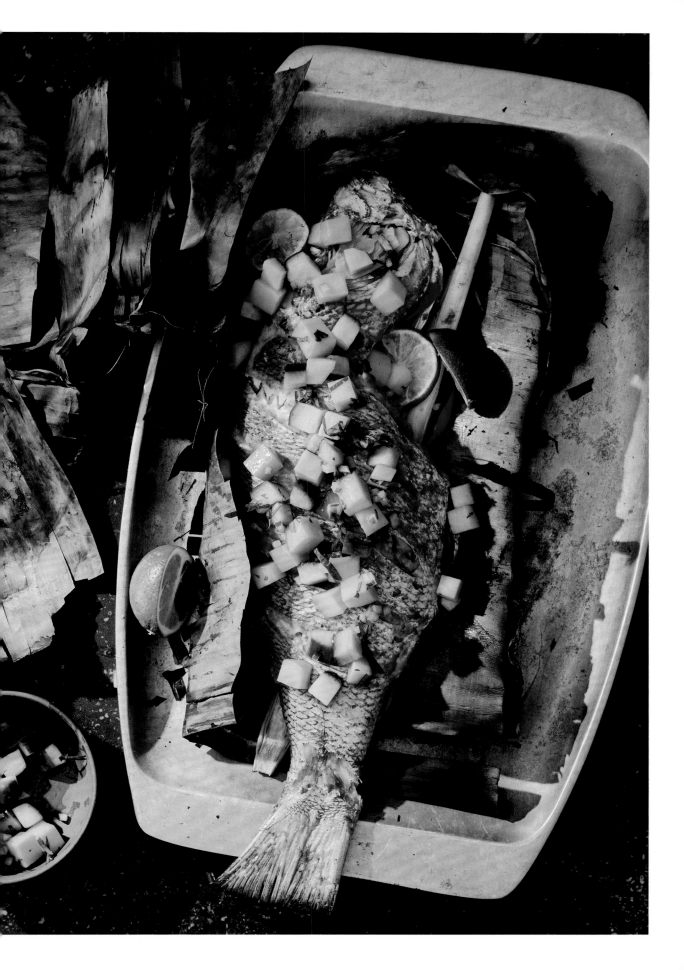

Cranberry Teriyaki Salmon with Shishitos and Sesame Brittle

We do a lot of entertaining at our cottage with friends and family. Cooking at the cottage is different from in the city. It is fun, simple and laid-back. No one should have to spend all of their time in the kitchen.

This salmon recipe packs in the wow factor, lakeside or back at home. It is so simple and does not require any lengthy marinating, but is super flavourful. The salmon turns out flaky, juicy and delicious with the homemade teriyaki sauce with cranberries and ginger, and it's taken up a notch with a nutty sesame seed brittle and blistered shishito peppers.

You can replace the sesame seeds with any toasted nut, coarsely chopped. Almonds are a great replacement.

MAKE THE SESAME BRITTLE

1. Preheat the oven to 350°F. Line a baking sheet with parchment paper.
2. In a small bowl, whisk the egg white until slightly foamy. Whisk in the sugar, salt, fennel and coriander. Add the sesame seeds and toss to coat. Spoon the sesame mixture in clumps onto the prepared baking sheet and bake, stirring occasionally, until golden brown, 10 to 12 minutes. Let cool. Break into small bite-size pieces. Store in an airtight container at room temperature for up to 2 weeks.

MAKE THE CRANBERRY TERIYAKI GLAZE

3. In a small saucepan, stir together the ingredients and bring to a boil over medium heat. When the mixture reaches a boil, reduce the heat and simmer until the glaze is thick and shiny, about 4 minutes. Let cool.

MARINATE AND BAKE THE SALMON

4. Line a baking sheet with parchment paper. Place the salmon skin side down on the prepared sheet. Season with salt and pepper. Spread half of the cranberry teriyaki glaze over the salmon, cover with plastic wrap and marinate in the refrigerator for at least 1 hour or overnight.
5. Preheat the oven to 375°F. Remove the plastic wrap and bake the salmon until flaky and cooked through, 20 to 24 minutes. (Bake times will depend on the thickness of the salmon.)
6. While the salmon is baking, bring the remaining glaze to a boil over high heat. When the glaze reaches a boil, reduce the heat and simmer, stirring occasionally, until slightly thickened, about 2 minutes. Remove from the heat.
7. Heat a large skillet over high heat. Add the olive oil and shishito peppers. Toss for 1 to 2 minutes, until starting to blister. Add the garlic, rosemary and thyme and cook for another minute. Remove from the heat. Discard the rosemary and thyme sprigs. Season with sea salt.
8. To serve, transfer the baked salmon to a serving platter. Brush with the remaining glaze, then sprinkle with the sliced green onions, sesame brittle and shishito peppers.

SERVES 4 TO 6

Sesame Brittle (makes ¾ cup)
1 large egg white
3 tablespoons granulated sugar
½ teaspoon kosher salt
¼ teaspoon coarsely ground fennel seeds
¼ teaspoon coarsely ground coriander seeds
1 cup sesame seeds

Cranberry Teriyaki Glaze
¼ cup dried cranberries
¼ cup soy sauce
2 tablespoons brown sugar
2 tablespoons honey
½ teaspoon sesame oil
2 cloves garlic, minced
2 teaspoons minced peeled fresh ginger
Zest and juice of 1 orange
1 tablespoon lemon juice

Salmon
1 skin-on salmon fillet (2 to 3 pounds/900 g to 1.4 kg)
Kosher salt and freshly ground black pepper
2 tablespoons olive oil
1 to 1½ cups shishito peppers
1 clove garlic, thinly sliced
1 sprig fresh rosemary
2 sprigs fresh thyme
Sea salt

For serving
1 bunch of green onions, thinly sliced on the diagonal
½ cup Sesame Brittle (recipe above)

EAT WITH
Creamy Spinach Parmesan Orzo (page 165)
+
Tempura Broccolini with Curry Leaf Mayonnaise (page 190)

Dukkah Trout with Hummus and Tomato Mint Chutney

With its colourful patterned skin and coral-coloured flesh, rainbow trout is a stunning fish that deserves to be showcased any night of the week. Pressing our Middle Eastern Dukkah Spice into the trout creates a toasted nutty crust that helps seal all the moisture in, resulting in tender fish with an exhilarating crunchy finish. Hummus, tomato mint chutney and fresh mint are the perfect accompaniments for the addictive dukkah, with its savoury sesame seeds, warm spices and earthy, crunchy roasted nuts.

MAKE THE HERB SAUCE

1. Place the ingredients in a blender. Purée until very smooth, adding a little water if necessary. Season with salt and pepper. Use immediately or store in an airtight container in the refrigerator for up to 2 weeks.

MAKE THE HUMMUS

2. Place the chickpeas and garlic in a food processor and blend until a rough paste is formed. With the machine running, add the tahini, olive oil, lemon zest and juice and process until silky smooth. Season with salt and pepper. Use immediately or store in an airtight container in the refrigerator for up to 1 week.

MAKE THE TOMATO MINT CHUTNEY

3. In a small bowl, combine the raisins and apple cider vinegar. Let stand until plumped, about 10 minutes.
4. Meanwhile, in a medium saucepan, heat the canola oil over medium heat. When the oil is hot, add the shallots, garlic and ginger and cook, stirring occasionally, until softened and just starting to brown, about 5 minutes. Add the tomato paste and cook, stirring, until the vegetables are evenly coated, about 1 minute.
5. Add the tomato purée, diced tomato, sun-dried tomatoes, brown sugar and the raisins and their vinegar. Bring to a boil over high heat, then reduce the heat to medium and simmer, stirring frequently, until thickened, about 15 minutes. Stir in the cherry tomatoes and mint. Season with salt and pepper. Remove from the heat and let cool.

COOK THE DUKKAH TROUT

6. Season the trout with salt and pepper and coat both sides of each fillet generously with 2 tablespoons of the dukkah spice. Heat the olive oil in a large nonstick skillet over medium heat. When the oil is hot, lay the fish in the pan and cook, turning once, until golden brown and the fish flakes easily with a fork, 3 to 4 minutes per side.
7. Spread the hummus and herb sauce on opposite sides of a serving platter. Transfer the fish on top of the sauces and spoon the tomato mint chutney over the fish. Garnish with mint leaves.

EAT WITH
Caponata Salad with Pepper and Aubergine Relish (page 117)
+
Leek and Spinach Pie (page 193)

SERVES 4 TO 6

Herb Sauce (makes 1 cup)
1 cup loosely packed fresh cilantro leaves
1 cup loosely packed fresh flat-leaf parsley leaves
1 cup loosely packed fresh mint leaves
1 (1-inch) piece peeled fresh ginger
Zest and juice of 1 lemon
1 tablespoon apple cider vinegar
3 tablespoons white miso
3 tablespoons tahini
2 tablespoons olive oil
1 tablespoon honey
Kosher salt and freshly ground black pepper

Hummus (makes 2 cups)
2 cups canned chickpeas, drained and rinsed
2 large cloves garlic, roughly chopped
¼ cup tahini
¼ cup olive oil
Zest and juice of 1 lemon
Kosher salt and freshly ground black pepper

Tomato Mint Chutney (makes 2 cups)
3 tablespoons raisins
3 tablespoons apple cider vinegar
2 tablespoons canola oil
2 shallots, thinly sliced
2 cloves garlic, thinly sliced
2 teaspoons grated peeled fresh ginger
1 tablespoon tomato paste
1 cup tomato purée
1 medium tomato, diced
¼ cup sun-dried tomatoes, thinly sliced
2 tablespoons brown sugar
1 cup cherry tomatoes, cut in half
½ cup roughly chopped fresh mint leaves
Kosher salt and freshly ground black pepper

Dukkah Trout
4 to 6 skinless trout fillets (5 to 6 ounces/140 to 170 g each)
Kosher salt and freshly ground black pepper
½ cup Dukkah Spice (page 227 or store-bought)
3 tablespoons olive oil
Fresh mint leaves, for garnish

Creole Shrimp and Grits with Sweet Corn Maque Choux

You do not need to take a trip to Louisiana to savour the flavours of the South. All that is required is fresh, plump shrimp and some bold spices. Paired with soft, creamy grits and sweet corn maque choux (pronounced *mock shoe* and similar to a succotash), this dish with a kick will quickly become a favourite. It is down-home comfort food at its finest. As they say in New Orleans, *laissez les bons temps rouler*, or let the good times roll!

Grits come in both yellow and white varieties. Our favourite is Bob's Red Mill white corn grits. The white makes a dramatic backdrop for the plump shrimp and accompaniments.

MAKE THE SWEET CORN MAQUE CHOUX

1. Heat a large saucepan over medium heat. Add the bacon and cook until it becomes nice and crispy, about 8 minutes. Stir in the corn kernels, onion, shallots, jalapeño, bell pepper and Cajun spice. Cook, stirring often, until the vegetables soften, about 10 minutes. Add the cream and warm through, stirring occasionally, for about 2 minutes. Remove from the heat.

MAKE THE WHITE CORN CHEESY GRITS

2. In a medium saucepan, combine the milk, water and salt and bring to a boil. When the mixture reaches a boil, whisk in the corn grits in a steady stream, then reduce the heat to low and cook, stirring occasionally, until the grits are creamy, about 5 minutes. Remove from the heat, stir in the cheese and season with salt and pepper. Cover and keep warm.

MAKE THE LEMON GARLIC SHRIMP

3. Melt the butter in a large skillet over medium-high heat. Stir in the lemon purée and confit garlic. Add the shrimp and cook until pink and the tails start to curl, 1 to 2 minutes per side. Remove from the heat and season with the lemon juice, Cajun spice, parsley, dill and green onions.

4. To serve, pour the cheesy grits into a large serving bowl. Arrange the shrimp on top of the grits and garnish with the sweet corn maque choux.

EAT WITH
Sweet Onion Cornbread (page 150)
+
Zucchini Parmesan Fritters with Hot Chili Honey (page 194)

SERVES 4 TO 6

Sweet Corn Maque Choux
2 slices bacon, diced
3 cups fresh corn kernels (from about 4 cobs)
1 medium yellow onion, chopped (about 1 cup)
2 shallots, finely diced
½ to 1 jalapeño pepper, seeded and finely diced
1 red bell pepper, chopped (about 1 cup)
2 teaspoons Cajun Spice (page 227 or store-bought)
½ cup heavy (35%) cream

White Corn Cheesy Grits
2 cups whole milk
1 cup water
1 teaspoon kosher salt, more for seasoning
1 cup white corn grits
1 cup grated white cheddar cheese
Freshly ground black pepper

Lemon Garlic Shrimp
4 tablespoons unsalted butter
1 teaspoon Lemon Purée (page 235) or (zest and juice of ½ lemon)
1 tablespoon Confit Garlic (page 233) or (1 clove garlic, chopped)
1 pound (450 g) medium shrimp (size 13–15), head-on, peeled and deveined
Juice of 1 lemon
1 teaspoon Cajun Spice (page 227 or store-bought)
1 tablespoon chopped fresh flat-leaf parsley
1 tablespoon chopped fresh dill
1 tablespoon chopped green onions

Lobster Thermidor

There is nothing better than East Coast lobster, especially when it finds its way into lobster Thermidor. This decadent creamy, cheesy French dish boasts a saucy mix of big chunks of lobster, cream, Gruyère cheese and brandy packed into a lobster shell. We top it with more cheese and broil it until it is lusciously bubbly and brown. Though surprisingly simple to make, it never fails to impress.

Put a cloth on it and eat swiftly: Store your lobsters in a bowl in the fridge with a damp cloth over them and they will go to sleep. Do not keep them alive for too long. Cook the lobsters on the day you buy them.

COOK THE LOBSTERS

1. Bring a large pot of salted water to a boil. When the water is boiling, add the lobsters and boil for 5 to 7 minutes until just cooked. Drain the lobsters and shock them under cold running water to cool down the meat. Cut each lobster in half lengthwise. Remove and crack the claws. Remove the meat from the claws, knuckles and bodies and cut into chunks. Discard any remaining lobster innards. Set the meat and shells aside.

MEANWHILE, MAKE THE PARMESAN BREADCRUMB TOPPING

2. While the lobster is cooking, melt the butter in a small saucepan over medium heat. Remove from the heat and stir in the breadcrumbs, Parmesan, parsley and salt. Set aside.

MAKE THE SAUCE

3. Melt the butter with the olive oil in a large, heavy saucepan over medium heat. Add the shallot and leek and cook, stirring occasionally, until soft, about 5 minutes. Add the mushrooms, season with salt and pepper, and continue cooking for 2 to 3 minutes until slightly caramelized. Deglaze the pan with the brandy. Stir in the cream, mustard and nutmeg and cook, stirring occasionally, until the sauce has thickened slightly, 3 to 4 minutes. Add the lobster meat and gently stir together and cook until the lobster is heated through. Remove from the heat, add the cheese and parsley, and stir until the cheese is melted. Taste and adjust seasoning as needed.
4. Set the oven to broil. Divide the lobster sauce between the shells. Sprinkle the Parmesan breadcrumbs over the sauce. Transfer the shells to a baking sheet and broil the lobster halves until golden brown, 2 to 3 minutes. Serve on a warm serving platter.

SERVES 4

2 live lobsters (about 1½ pounds/675 g each)

Parmesan Breadcrumb Topping
2 tablespoons unsalted butter
¾ cup panko breadcrumbs
2 tablespoons grated Parmesan cheese
1 tablespoon chopped fresh flat-leaf parsley
½ teaspoon kosher salt

Sauce
2 tablespoons unsalted butter
1 tablespoon olive oil
2 tablespoons minced shallot
1 large leek (white and light green parts only), cut in half lengthwise and thinly sliced
1 cup quartered button mushrooms
Kosher salt and freshly ground black pepper
2 ounces brandy
1½ cups heavy (35%) cream
2 teaspoons Dijon mustard
Pinch of nutmeg
½ cup grated Gruyère cheese
1 tablespoon chopped fresh flat-leaf parsley

EAT WITH
Asparagus with Citrus, Anchovy and Almond Butter (page 153)
+
Sunchokes Bravas with Chorizo and Romesco Sauce (page 189)

Tuna Poke Tostadas

We love a good tuna taco as much as anyone, but tostadas are fun, too. Hawaii is a favourite travel destination for us. This tuna poke tostada is our version of the ones we enjoyed at beachside food trucks in Maui. It has a deeply satisfying crunchy base and tantalizing toppings—Pineapple Salted Caper Salsa, Nori Guacamole and Seaweed Salad. Taco Tuesdays are now Tostada Tuesdays at our house. More accurately, a flavour-packed party suitable for every day of the week.

If you do not have tostadas, swap in tacos or tortillas or turn all the fixins into a fantastic poke salad bowl.

MAKE THE PICKLES

1. In a small saucepan, combine the rice vinegar, sugar and salt. Cook over medium-high heat, stirring, until the mixture reaches a simmer.
2. Place the red onion and radishes in a 2-cup mason jar. Pour the hot vinegar mixture over the onion and radishes, seal with the lid and give the jar a quick shake. Let the onions and radishes marinate for 30 minutes. Serve immediately or store in the refrigerator for up to 2 weeks.

MAKE THE PINEAPPLE SALTED CAPER SALSA

3. In a medium bowl, stir together the red onion, chili and lime juice. Let sit for 5 minutes. Stir in the pineapple, cilantro and capers. Season to taste with additional lime juice or salt. Serve immediately or store, covered, in the refrigerator for up to 2 days.

MAKE THE SEAWEED SALAD

4. Place the seaweed in a medium bowl and cover with cold water. Let the seaweed rehydrate for 10 minutes.
5. In another medium bowl, whisk together the soy sauce, rice vinegar, mirin, sesame oil, sesame seeds, sugar, ginger and green onions.
6. Drain the seaweed in a colander and rinse it thoroughly. Squeeze as much water out of it as you can. Add the rehydrated seaweed to the dressing and toss to coat evenly. Adjust the seasonings to taste. Serve immediately or store, covered, in the refrigerator for up to 2 days.

MAKE THE NORI GUACAMOLE

7. In a small bowl, stir together the red onion and lime juice. Let sit for 5 minutes.
8. Cut the avocados in half lengthwise and remove the pits. Using a spoon, scoop out the flesh and transfer to the bowl. Add the jalapeño and cilantro and stir together. Season with the crumbled nori, togarashi and salt. Cover and refrigerate until ready to serve.

Recipe continues . . .

SERVES 4 TO 6

Pickles
¾ cup rice wine vinegar
2 tablespoons granulated sugar
1 teaspoon fine sea salt
½ cup very thinly sliced red onion
½ cup very thinly sliced radishes

Pineapple Salted Caper Salsa (makes 2½ cups)
¼ cup finely diced red onion
½ to 1 Fresno chili, thinly sliced
3 tablespoons lime juice, more as needed
2 cups diced fresh pineapple
¼ cup packed fresh cilantro leaves, chopped
2 tablespoons salted unrinsed capers, chopped
Kosher salt

Seaweed Salad (makes about ½ cup)
2 ounces (57 g) dried mixed seaweed (wakame, arame or hijiki)
3 tablespoons soy sauce
2 tablespoons seasoned rice vinegar
2 tablespoons mirin
1 teaspoon sesame oil
1 tablespoon toasted sesame seeds
1 tablespoon granulated sugar
1 teaspoon grated peeled fresh ginger
2 green onions, finely chopped

Nori Guacamole (makes 2 cups)
½ red onion, finely diced
2 tablespoons lime juice
2 avocados
1 jalapeño pepper, seeded and minced
2 tablespoons chopped fresh cilantro leaves
2 sheets nori, crumbled
Togarashi, to taste
Kosher salt

Recipe continued from previous page . . .

PREPARE THE TUNA

9. In a medium bowl, combine the cubed tuna, soy sauce, rice vinegar, mirin, sesame oil, sambal oelek and ginger. Gently toss together. Adjust the seasoning as desired. Cover and refrigerate until ready to serve.

10. To serve, transfer the tuna to a bowl and nestle it in a larger bowl of ice. Arrange the tuna, tostadas, pickles, pineapple salted caper salsa, seaweed salad and nori guacamole on the table and allow your guests to create their own tostadas.

EAT WITH
Baked Sweet Potatoes with Chipotle Lime Crema, Bacon, Pecans and
Rosemary Honey (page 137)
+
Honey Mustard Carrot Slaw (page 133)
+/or
Apple and Fennel Cabbage Slaw (page 133)

Tuna

1 pound (450 g) albacore tuna, cut into cubes

¼ cup soy sauce, more to taste

2 tablespoons rice wine vinegar

2 tablespoons mirin

2 teaspoons sesame oil

2 teaspoons sambal oelek

1½ teaspoons grated peeled fresh ginger

8 corn tostadas, for serving

Miso Black Cod with Mushroom Soy Broth

We spent many fabulous years living and working in New York City and have taken a lot of inspiration from its many incredible restaurants. This dish, inspired by one of our go-tos, is our take on elevated fish and chips, and it brings back wonderful memories. The buttery cod is marinated in a bath of Asian flavours and takes on a thunderbolt of umami when served with umami aioli, crispy tempura mushrooms and poached bok choy.

Black cod, or sablefish, sometimes is not easy to find. A fish we will substitute is salmon. For a real treat, ask your fishmonger if they would part with the "toro," or belly meat, of the salmon. It's higher in fat, has great flavour and is packed with protein and omega-3 fats.

MAKE THE UMAMI AIOLI

1. In a small food processor or blender, combine the egg yolks, rice wine vinegar, lemon juice, soy sauce and mustard. Process until well blended.
2. With the motor running, add the mushroom powder, then the canola oil and olive oil in a slow, steady stream and process until emulsified, about 2 minutes. Season with salt and pepper. Use immediately or transfer to an airtight container and refrigerate for up to 2 weeks.

MARINATE THE MISO BLACK COD

3. In a small saucepan, bring the mirin and sake to a boil over high heat. When the mixture is boiling, add the brown sugar and stir until dissolved. Remove from the heat and whisk in the miso. Let cool completely.
4. Place the black cod in a nonreactive container just large enough to fit it, and cover with the marinade. Cover and refrigerate for at least 4 hours or ideally overnight.

MAKE THE MUSHROOM SOY BROTH

5. Heat the mushroom stock in a large saucepan over medium heat. Add the button and enoki mushrooms, bok choy and chili and simmer for 10 minutes. Add the cilantro and green onions. Season to taste with soy sauce. Keep hot until ready to serve.

COOK THE BLACK COD

6. Place an oven rack in the lowest position so the fish does not brown too quickly. Set the oven to broil. Line a baking sheet with foil.
7. Remove the fish from the marinade and lightly wipe off any excess marinade. Place the fish skin side down on the prepared baking sheet and broil until almost opaque throughout, 8 to 10 minutes.

Recipe continues . . .

SERVES 4 TO 6

Umami Aioli (makes about 1½ cups)
3 large egg yolks, at room temperature
2 tablespoons rice wine vinegar
1 tablespoon lemon juice
1 tablespoon soy sauce
1 teaspoon Dijon mustard
2 teaspoons Mushroom Powder (page 235)
1 cup canola oil
¼ cup extra-virgin olive oil
Kosher salt and freshly ground black pepper

Miso Black Cod
¼ cup mirin
¼ cup sake
2 tablespoons brown sugar
½ cup white miso
4 to 6 skinless black cod fillets, about 1½ inches thick (6 ounces/170 g each)

Mushroom Soy Broth
4 cups mushroom or Vegetable Stock (page 238 or store-bought)
8 ounces (225 g) button mushrooms, sliced (about 2 cups)
1 package (3½ ounces/100 g) enoki mushrooms, bottoms removed, cut into 1-inch pieces
12 pieces baby bok choy, quartered or cut in half
¼ Fresno chili, thinly sliced
2 tablespoons chopped fresh cilantro
2 green onions, sliced
Soy sauce

Recipe continued from previous page . . .

MAKE THE TEMPURA ENOKI MUSHROOMS

8. In a medium bowl, whisk together the flour, cornstarch and salt. Whisk in the sparkling water until just combined.

9. Line a plate with paper towel. In a deep medium saucepan, heat 4 inches of vegetable oil to 365°F over medium heat. Working in batches, dip the enoki mushrooms in the batter, let the excess drip back into the bowl, then gently place the mushrooms in the hot oil. Cook turning after a minute or so until golden, about 3 minutes in total. Using tongs, transfer the mushrooms to the paper towel to drain and sprinkle lightly with salt. Serve immediately.

10. To serve, spoon a bed of the bok choy and mushrooms into shallow serving bowls. Top with the fish. Pour the hot mushroom soy broth over the top. Top the fish with a tablespoon of the umami aioli and heat with a kitchen torch until the aioli caramelizes. Serve with the tempura enoki mushrooms and more umami aioli on the side.

EAT WITH
Blistered Beans with Ginger, Black Garlic and Cashews (page 154)
+
Hoisin-Glazed Eggplant with Sesame Miso Baba Ganoush (page 170)

Tempura Enoki Mushrooms

1 cup all-purpose flour
¼ cup cornstarch
½ teaspoon sea salt, more for garnish
1¼ cups sparkling water (or a combination of beer and sparkling water), chilled
Vegetable oil, for deep-frying
2 packages (3½ ounces/100 g each) enoki mushrooms, bottoms trimmed, kept in cluster

MEAT

Oven-Braised Barbecue Beef Brisket with Caramelized Onion Jus

Brisket is the cornerstone of Texas barbecue, but you do not have to travel to the Lone Star State to get your hands on this drool-inducing beef. This cut of meat loves low and slow cooking, so while it may take a bit of time, it yields phenomenal results with little effort. That is why it is so beloved by chefs and home cooks alike. Rubbed with a generous amount of barbecue spice and ground espresso, then braised with onions, chipotle peppers and aromatics loaded with incredible depth of flavour, this brisket is so tender and oozing with smoky flavour that your guests will never guess it was not cooked on the grill.

This recipe calls for a large brisket, so you'll have plenty of leftovers. We recommend pairing with eggs, incorporating into hash browns or tucking thick slices into a couple of cheesy pull-apart rolls (page 149) for the most luscious snack ever.

1. In a small bowl, combine the soy sauce, honey, hearth barbecue spice rub, brown sugar, espresso, mustard, chipotle peppers and garlic. Stir well. Place the brisket in a roasting pan and coat well with the marinade. Cover and refrigerate for at least 2 hours or overnight.
2. Preheat the oven to 325°F.
3. Remove the brisket from the marinade and place on a baking sheet or platter. Discard the marinade. Return the brisket to the roasting pan and bring to room temperature.
4. In a large skillet over medium-high heat, melt the butter in the olive oil. Add the onions and cook, stirring occasionally, until caramelized, 15 to 20 minutes. Add the beef stock, apple cider vinegar, tomatoes, rosemary and thyme. Bring to a boil, then reduce the heat and simmer for 5 minutes. Pour the sauce over the brisket. Cover the roasting pan with foil and bake until the brisket is tender, 3½ to 4 hours.
5. Carefully remove the brisket and onions from the sauce and transfer to a rimmed baking sheet. Strain the sauce into a medium saucepan. Skim off excess fat and discard. Reduce the liquid over high heat until the sauce thickens. Add the onions and parsley to the sauce.
6. Slice the brisket thinly against the grain and arrange on a serving platter. Serve with the caramelized onion jus on the side.

SERVES 6 TO 8

- ½ cup soy sauce
- ¼ cup honey
- ¼ cup Hearth Barbecue Spice Rub (page 229)
- 2 tablespoons brown sugar
- 2 tablespoons finely ground espresso
- 2 tablespoons Dijon mustard
- 1 tablespoon minced chipotle peppers in adobo sauce
- 3 cloves garlic, minced
- 1 beef brisket roast (5 pounds/2.25 kg)
- 2 tablespoons unsalted butter
- 1 tablespoon olive oil
- 4 white onions, peeled and quartered
- 3 cups beef stock
- ¼ cup apple cider vinegar
- 1 can (19 ounces/540 mL) chopped tomatoes
- 2 sprigs fresh rosemary
- 4 sprigs fresh thyme
- 2 tablespoons chopped fresh flat-leaf parsley

EAT WITH
Baked Sweet Potatoes with Chipotle Lime Crema, Bacon, Pecans and Rosemary Honey (page 137)
+
Cheesy Garlic Pull-Apart Bread (page 149)
+
Corn, Zucchini and Cheddar Sauté (page 162)

Cottage Ribs with Soy Ginger Marinade

If you are a fan of Korean food, you have probably heard of galbi, a popular dish of sliced beef short ribs marinated in a sweet-and-savoury barbecue-style marinade and then grilled. Thin crosscut short ribs are a cottage staple that translate seamlessly to city life because they cook quickly on a hot grill or under the broiler, and all the work is in the marinade. This is an effortless yet delicious meal to whip up, whether you're at the cottage or at home.

When shopping for beef short ribs, look for well-marbled ribs for extra tenderness and flavour.

1. In a large bowl, combine the soy sauce, Worcestershire sauce, sesame oil, brown sugar, mustard, gochujang, garlic, ginger and lime zest and juice. Whisk together well. Add the ribs, pushing the meat down into the marinade, and mix well. Cover and marinate in the refrigerator for 1 to 2 hours.
2. Prepare the grill for direct cooking over medium-high heat (or position a rack 4 to 6 inches under the broiler and set the oven to broil).
3. Remove the ribs from the marinade. Pour the marinade into a small pot, add the honey and bring to a boil over medium heat. Remove from the heat.
4. Grill the ribs (or broil on a baking sheet lined with foil), basting with the marinade while cooking, until the meat is cooked and lightly caramelized with grill marks, about 2 minutes per side.
5. Transfer the ribs to a serving platter. Drizzle with some of the remaining marinade and garnish with the green onions and sesame seeds.

EAT WITH
Crispy Smashed Potatoes with Caramelized Onion Dip (page 138)
+
Savoy Cabbage with Shiitake Mushrooms, Sausage, Miso and Garlic
(page 185)

SERVES 4 TO 6

½ cup soy sauce
1 tablespoon Worcestershire sauce
1 tablespoon sesame oil
2 tablespoons brown sugar
2 tablespoons Dijon mustard
2 tablespoons gochujang
1 tablespoon chopped garlic
1 tablespoon chopped peeled fresh ginger
Zest and juice of 1 lime
2 to 3 pounds (900 g to 1.4 kg) thinly sliced beef ribs (Miami or Korean-style)
2 tablespoons honey

Garnishes

1 bunch of green onions, thinly sliced on the diagonal
1 tablespoon toasted sesame seeds

Mongolian Beef Stir-Fry with Mushroom XO Sauce

You have probably made stir-fries many times, but they probably were nothing like this one. Consider this your new favourite stir-fry, with its zippy Mushroom XO Sauce. There is no need to order in! This easy 30-minute recipe is fresh, flavourful and ready to go in a hurry—a relief from the frenzied scramble to get something on the table quickly.

We like beef tenderloin in this dish, but you can you can use a less expensive cut such as flank or sirloin steak.

1. Bring a large pot of salted water to a boil over high heat. Have ready a large bowl of ice water. When the water is boiling, add the broccoli florets and cook until bright green, about 2 minutes. Drain the broccoli and immediately plunge into the ice water. Drain well and set aside.

2. Heat a large skillet over medium-high heat. Add 1 tablespoon of the canola oil, the red and yellow bell peppers and red onion and cook, stirring together, until just tender, 3 to 4 minutes. Transfer the peppers and onions to a large plate.

3. Season the beef with salt and pepper. Return the skillet to high heat, then add 1 tablespoon of the canola oil and half of the beef and cook, stirring frequently, until the meat is browned, 2 to 3 minutes. Transfer the beef to the plate with the peppers and onions. Repeat with the remaining beef and 1 tablespoon of the canola oil.

4. To the same pan, over medium-high heat, add the remaining 1 tablespoon canola oil, garlic, ginger and chilies and cook, stirring, for 30 seconds. Add the pepper and beef mixture, broccoli and green onions and toss together well.

5. In a small bowl, whisk together the mushroom stock, soy sauce, cornstarch and brown sugar. Add to the skillet, stir, and bring to a simmer. Cook until the sauce has thickened, 2 to 3 minutes.

6. Serve the beef stir-fry on top of steamed jasmine rice on a serving platter, garnished with the crispy shallots and mushroom XO sauce.

SERVES 4 TO 6

2 cups broccoli florets
4 tablespoons canola oil, divided
1 red bell pepper, cut into strips
1 yellow bell pepper, cut into strips
1 red onion, sliced
1 pound (450 g) beef tenderloin, thinly sliced against the grain and cut into strips
Kosher salt and freshly ground black pepper
2 tablespoons minced garlic
2 tablespoons minced peeled fresh ginger
½ Fresno chili, thinly sliced
1 bunch of green onions, cut on the diagonal into 2-inch pieces
½ cup mushroom or beef stock or water
¼ cup soy sauce
2 tablespoons cornstarch
2 teaspoons brown sugar

For serving

Steamed jasmine rice
½ cup Crispy Fried Shallots (page 232)
Mushroom XO Sauce (page 241)

EAT WITH
Hoisin-Glazed Eggplant with Sesame Miso Baba Ganoush (page 170)
+
Shrimp and Egg Fried Rice (page 142) instead of steamed jasmine rice

Asado Grilled Flank Steak with Steak Sauces

This recipe was inspired by Argentinian asados, which are similar to what we know as a barbecue but are so much more. Asados are a social event, and you will find lots of families and friends hanging out enjoying tasty treats coming right off the grill.

Sebastian Cortez is the owner of Sebastian & Co Fine Meats in Vancouver. A professional chef turned butcher, he takes his inspiration from the artisan butcher shops of Europe and South America. His passion for food and fine meats is clear the moment you step into his shop. Sebastian also has small-batch artisan products line. The only reason why this steak tastes as good as it does is his charcoal rub. We do not have the recipe and would never ask. Instead, we just order it online from our dear friend with all of the other products he makes. Visit sebastianandco.ca and treat yourself to a wicked pantry staple, then fire up the grill!

1. In a large bowl, stir together the soy sauce, mustard, thyme, paprika and garlic. Add the flank steak and turn to thoroughly coat with the marinade. Cover with plastic wrap and marinate in the refrigerator for at least 1 hour or up to 4 hours.
2. Prepare the grill for direct cooking over high heat.
3. Remove the steak from the marinade and discard the marinade. Season the steak with half of the charcoal rub. Grill the steak, without moving it, for 5 to 8 minutes, then turn and sear for another 5 minutes or until desired doneness is reached. Remove the steak from the grill and let rest for 10 minutes.
4. Sprinkle the remaining charcoal rub on both sides of the steak. Thinly slice the steak against the grain. Transfer to a serving platter and serve topped with chimichurri sauce and AP steak sauce.

SERVES 4 TO 6

¼ cup soy sauce
2 tablespoons Dijon mustard
2 teaspoons fresh thyme leaves
1 teaspoon smoked paprika
2 cloves garlic, minced
1 flank steak (2 pounds/900 g)
3 to 4 tablespoons Sebastian & Co Charcoal Rub (or season steak with kosher salt and freshly ground black pepper)

For serving
Chimichurri Sauce (page 239)
AP Steak Sauce (page 238 or store-bought)

EAT WITH
Baked Sweet Potatoes with Chipotle Lime Crema, Bacon, Pecans and Rosemary Honey (page 137)
+
Brussels Sprouts, Bacon and Toasted Fregola (page 157)

Ras el Hanout Spiced Roast Leg of Lamb with Mint Pomegranate Yogurt

Our lamb roast with aromatic ras el hanout and an easy-to-make mint pomegranate yogurt is a spicy alternative to a traditional roast lamb and delivers rich Middle Eastern flavours.

The Moroccan spice mix ras el hanout gets its name from the Arabic phrase for "top of the shop" or "top shelf," so you know it is good. It's a complex mix usually made from a dozen or more deeply flavourful, rich spices—traditionally the best spices the spice merchant has to offer. It has an almost curry-like flavour that makes whatever it touches incredibly flavourful, and it is delicious rubbed on lamb, fish and chicken.

The mint pomegranate Moroccan-spiced yogurt is just as awesome served with vegetables, fish or chicken.

MAKE THE MINT POMEGRANATE YOGURT

1. In a small bowl, whisk together the ingredients. Season with salt and pepper. Store, covered, in the refrigerator for up to 1 week.

MARINATE THE LAMB

2. In a small bowl, combine the olive oil, anchovies, pomegranate molasses, orange purée, lemon purée, ras el hanout, garlic, capers, mustard, parsley, rosemary and thyme. Stir together to form a loose paste. Lay the lamb in a large baking dish and rub the marinade on both sides and inside where the bone was removed. Cover and marinate in the refrigerator for at least 3 hours or ideally overnight.

ROAST THE LAMB

3. Preheat the oven to 450°F.
4. Remove the lamb from the refrigerator and let stand at room temperature for about 1 hour. Season the entire leg with salt and pepper. Lay the lamb, fat side up, on a rack in a large roasting pan and roast for 15 minutes. Reduce the heat to 350°F and continue to roast the lamb until a thermometer inserted into the thickest part of the leg registers 125 to 130°F, about 1 hour, depending on the size of the leg. Transfer the lamb to a cutting board and let rest for 20 minutes.
5. Using a sharp carving knife, thinly slice the lamb. Serve on a platter with the mint pomegranate yogurt on the side.

EAT WITH
Leek and Spinach Pie (page 193)
+
Moroccan Couscous (page 146)

SERVES 6 TO 8

Mint Pomegranate Yogurt (makes about 1½ cups)
1 cup plain full-fat Greek yogurt
¼ cup pomegranate seeds
2 tablespoons chopped fresh mint
1 tablespoon Dijon mustard
1 tablespoon honey
2 teaspoons pomegranate molasses
1 teaspoon Ras el Hanout Spice (page 230 or store-bought)
1 teaspoon orange zest
2 tablespoons orange juice
Kosher salt and freshly ground black pepper

Ras el Hanout Spiced Roast Leg of Lamb
½ cup olive oil
2 tablespoons finely chopped anchovies
2 tablespoons pomegranate molasses
2 tablespoons Orange Purée (page 236) or orange zest
1 tablespoon Lemon Purée (page 235) or lemon zest
1 tablespoon Ras el Hanout Spice (page 230 or store-bought)
1 tablespoon finely chopped garlic
1 tablespoon chopped drained capers
1 tablespoon Dijon mustard
2 tablespoons chopped fresh flat-leaf parsley
1 tablespoon chopped fresh rosemary
1 tablespoon chopped fresh thyme
1 boneless leg of lamb (5 to 6 pounds/2.25 to 2.7 kg)
Kosher salt and freshly ground black pepper

Braised Lamb Shanks with Fennel, Feta and Dill Salad

This dish comes together so easily. Slide it in the oven and it works its magic without your having to stand at the stove for hours—though it tastes like you did! That is because the rich flavours of the wine and caramelized fennel seep into the lamb, giving it a robust flavour that transports you to the coastlines of Greece.

Lamb shanks are usually less expensive than chops, so a good economical option. Select shanks that are pretty much the same size so they cook evenly. Gauge for roughly 1 pound (450 g) per person.

BRAISE THE LAMB SHANKS

1. Preheat the oven to 350°F.
2. Season the lamb shanks well with salt and pepper. In a large, heavy ovenproof pot, heat the olive oil over medium-high heat. Add the shanks to the pot and brown all sides until well caramelized, 10 to 12 minutes total. Transfer the shanks to a large plate.
3. Reduce the heat to medium. Add the carrots, celery, onion, fennel and garlic to the pot and cook, stirring occasionally, until the vegetables are tender and well caramelized, 10 to 12 minutes. Add the tomato paste and cook, stirring, for 2 minutes. Add the red wine and cook until reduced by half, 4 to 5 minutes. Add the chopped tomatoes and their liquid, beef stock, thyme and rosemary.
4. Return the lamb shanks to the pot. The lamb should be submerged; if it's not, add more stock or water. Bring to a boil and season with salt and pepper. Cover, place in the oven and cook until the meat is very tender, 2 to 2½ hours. Turn the shanks over about halfway through the cooking time.

MAKE THE FENNEL, FETA AND DILL SALAD

5. When the lamb is almost cooked, in a medium bowl, toss together the fennel, dill, olive oil and lemon juice. Just before serving, add the feta cheese and season well with salt and pepper.

FINISH THE BRAISED LAMB SHANKS

6. Using a slotted spoon, transfer the shanks to a warm serving bowl.
7. Spoon off as much fat as possible from the surface of the braising liquid. Remove and discard the thyme and rosemary sprigs. Strain the braising liquid into a small saucepan and reduce over medium-high heat until thickened slightly, about 5 minutes. Remove from the heat, whisk in the butter and season with salt and pepper.
8. To serve, spoon the sauce over the lamb shanks and top with the fennel, feta and dill salad.

EAT WITH
Fattoush Salad with Heirloom Tomatoes and Za'atar Pita Crisps (page 122)
+
Mushroom Risotto (page 145)

SERVES 4

Braised Lamb Shanks
4 large lamb shanks (1 to 1½ pounds/450 to 675 g each)
Kosher salt and freshly ground black pepper
2 tablespoons olive oil
2 carrots, peeled and diced
4 stalks celery, diced
1 large white onion, chopped
1 fennel bulb, cut into 2-inch cubes
4 to 6 cloves garlic, crushed
2 tablespoons tomato paste
2 cups dry red wine
1 can (28 ounces/796 mL) chopped tomatoes
4 cups beef stock
4 sprigs fresh thyme
2 sprigs fresh rosemary
2 tablespoons unsalted butter

Fennel, Feta and Dill Salad
2 small fennel bulbs, shaved lengthwise
½ cup chopped fresh dill
¼ cup olive oil
¼ cup lemon juice
⅓ cup crumbled feta cheese
Kosher salt and freshly ground black pepper

EAT WITH
Bacon and Egg Iceberg Salad with
Avocado Dressing (page 113)
+
Harissa-Roasted Parsnips with Whipped Feta,
Pistachios and Rosemary Honey (page 169)

Crown Roast of Lamb with Hollandaise Sauce

Crown roast of lamb is one of the most festive and delicious cuts of meat. This succulent roast is flavourful on its own but is robust enough that it pairs beautifully with the bold flavours in our marinade. Those briny olives, umami-packed sun-dried tomatoes and Provençale herbs and garlic only increase the deliciousness.

A well-rested piece of meat will be more tender and retain its juices better when you slice it.

MAKE THE CLARIFIED BUTTER

1. In a small saucepan, melt the butter over medium-high heat. As the butter approaches a boil, an even layer of white milk proteins will float to the surface. When the butter boils, the milk proteins will become foamy. Reduce the heat to medium and continue to gently boil; the milk proteins will break apart and eventually sink to the bottom, and the boiling will begin to calm and then cease. Once the boiling has stopped, pour the butter through a cheesecloth-lined strainer into a heatproof container. Discard the milk solids. Let cool, then transfer to an airtight container and store in the refrigerator for up to 2 months.

MAKE THE CROWN ROAST OF LAMB

2. Preheat the oven to 450°F.
3. Season the lamb all over with salt and pepper. Lay the racks of lamb in front of you horizontally, bone side up and with the frenched bones facing away from you. Make shallow ¼-inch-deep cuts through the meat between each bone.
4. Stand the racks of lamb up, with the meatiest portion of the meat facing inward, and shape the two racks into a circle. The frenched bones should curve outward to create the look of a crown. Using butcher's twine, tie once midway up the frenched bones and again below the bones in the meaty portion.
5. In a food processor, combine the olives, sun-dried tomatoes, lemon zest, mustard, garlic, thyme and rosemary. Pulse until finely chopped. While pulsing, add just enough olive oil to form a thick paste. Season the paste with salt and pepper.
6. Coat the racks of lamb all over with the marinade paste and set the lamb in a small round baking pan. Cover the frenched bones loosely with a sheet of foil to prevent them from burning. Place the pan in the oven and roast until the thickest part of the meat reaches an internal temperature of 130 to 135°F, for 30 to 35 minutes. Transfer the lamb to a serving platter and let rest for about 10 minutes.

MAKE THE HOLLANDAISE SAUCE

7. While the lamb is resting, make the hollandaise sauce. Place the egg yolks in a large bowl and whisk over a saucepan of simmering water until thickened, about 2 minutes. Remove from the heat and, while whisking, slowly add the clarified butter until emulsified. Season with lemon juice, Tabasco, Worcestershire sauce, and salt and pepper. Cover to keep warm.

FINISH THE CROWN ROAST OF LAMB

8. When ready to serve, remove the foil from the lamb and cut the string away from the roast. Fill the centre of the crown with the Moroccan couscous. Serve with the hollandaise sauce on the side.

SERVES 4 TO 6

Clarified Butter
½ pound (225 g) unsalted butter, cubed

Crown Roast of Lamb
2 lamb racks (1½ to 2 pounds/675 to 900 g each; 6 to 8 ribs per rack), trimmed and frenched
Kosher salt and freshly ground black pepper
¼ cup pitted Kalamata olives
3 tablespoons sun-dried tomatoes
1 teaspoon lemon zest
1 teaspoon Dijon mustard
2 cloves garlic, peeled
2 sprigs fresh thyme, leaves only
1 sprig fresh rosemary, leaves only
Olive oil
1 batch Moroccan Couscous (page 146)

Hollandaise Sauce
4 egg yolks
¾ cup warm Clarified Butter (recipe above)
1 tablespoon lemon juice
Dash of Tabasco
Dash of Worcestershire sauce
Kosher salt and freshly ground black pepper

Gochujang-Brined Rack of Pork with Apple Thyme Chutney

Pork chops are common on the dinner table, but rack of pork is often saved for special occasions. We are going to let you in on a secret. This bone-in cut is just as easy to cook as chops but makes for an outstanding presentation. Bonus, it is super easy to make, thanks to our brine and a few key ingredients. Marrying fragrant apple with heat from the fiery fermented gochujang paste and a touch of sweetness results in vibrant, concentrated flavours that will wow everyone.

Adjust the heat level by increasing or reducing the amount of gochujang you use. The brine is also fabulous with any cut of pork or chicken.

MAKE THE GOCHUJANG GLAZE
1. In a small saucepan, combine the ingredients and bring just to a simmer, stirring to dissolve the sugar. Reserve 3 tablespoon for the apple thyme chutney. Store in an airtight container in the refrigerator for up to 1 week.

MAKE THE APPLE THYME CHUTNEY
2. Heat the canola oil in a large skillet over medium-high heat. Add the shallots and cook, stirring occasionally, until caramelized, 2 to 3 minutes. Add the butter, apples, brown sugar, apple cider vinegar, mustard and thyme. Cook, stirring occasionally, until the apples are softened, 2 to 3 minutes. Stir in the reserved gochujang glaze and the chili flakes. Store in an airtight container in the refrigerator for up to 1 week.

BRINE THE RACK OF PORK
3. In a medium saucepan, combine 4 cups of the cold water with the salt, brown sugar, gochujang, black peppercorns, garlic, thyme and bay leaves. Bring to a boil over high heat, stirring until the sugar and salt dissolve.
4. Pour the brine into a wide pot or container large enough to hold the pork. Add the remaining 2 cups cold water and stir to blend. Let stand until the brine is cool to the touch, about 1 hour.
5. When the brine is cool, completely submerge the pork, using a plate or small pot as a weight, cover and refrigerate overnight.

ROAST THE RACK OF PORK
6. Preheat the oven to 450°F.
7. Remove the pork from the brine; discard the brine. Pat dry the pork with paper towel. In a roasting pan, combine the onion, carrot and celery. Season the pork well with salt and pepper and place the rack, fat side up, on the vegetables. Brush the rack with one-third of the gochujang glaze. Roast for 15 minutes. Reduce the heat to 325°F and continue to roast, periodically basting the pork with the remaining glaze, for 1½ to 2 hours, until a meat thermometer inserted into the centre of the pork registers 140°F. Remove from the oven and let rest for 10 minutes before carving.
8. Cut the rack into chops and arrange on a serving platter with the roasted vegetables. Serve with the apple thyme chutney.

SERVES 6

Gochujang Glaze
½ cup gochujang
2 tablespoons brown sugar
2 tablespoons soy sauce
2 tablespoons seasoned rice vinegar
2 teaspoons sesame oil

Apple Thyme Chutney (makes about 2 cups)
1 tablespoon canola oil
3 shallots, thinly sliced
2 tablespoons unsalted butter
2 Gala apples, cored and sliced
2 tablespoons brown sugar
2 tablespoons apple cider vinegar
1 tablespoon grainy mustard
1 teaspoon fresh thyme leaves
3 tablespoons reserved Gochujang Glaze (recipe above)
¼ teaspoon red chili flakes

Gochujang-Brined Rack of Pork
6 cups cold water, divided
½ cup kosher salt (we use Diamond Crystal)
½ cup packed brown sugar
3 tablespoons gochujang
1 teaspoon black peppercorns
1 head of garlic, cut in half crosswise
4 sprigs fresh thyme
2 bay leaves
1 centre-cut pork rib roast (5 to 6 pounds/2.25 to 2.7 kg), tied
1 small white onion, roughly chopped
1 large carrot, peeled and roughly chopped
2 stalks celery, roughly chopped
Kosher salt and freshly ground black pepper

EAT WITH
Gai Lan with Chili Jam (page 166)
+
Polenta with Butternut Squash, Swiss Chard and Mascarpone (page 174)

Honey-Garlic Ribs

This has to be the best and easiest way to make perfect, moist, fall-off-the-bone ribs with a honey-garlic sauce that is finger-licking good. The ribs in this recipe are baked, but they are delicious finished off on the barbecue as well. Make sure you slather them with lots of glaze.

You can braise the ribs and make the glaze up to 2 days ahead. Just cool the ribs and glaze down, cover and refrigerate.

START THE RIBS

1. Place the ribs in a large, heavy pot and cover with the onions, carrot, garlic, ginger and soy sauce. Add enough water to cover the ribs. Place the pot over medium-high heat and bring the liquid to a boil. When it comes to a boil, reduce the heat to low, cover and simmer until the ribs are tender, 1 to 1½ hours. Remove the ribs from the pot and discard the liquid and solids. Allow the ribs to cool.

MAKE THE HONEY-GARLIC GLAZE

2. When the ribs are cool, combine the ingredients in a small saucepan. Bring to a boil over medium-high heat, whisking together well, then reduce the heat and simmer until thickened slightly, 1 to 2 minutes. Remove from the heat.

BAKE THE RIBS

3. Preheat the oven to 450°F. Line a baking sheet with foil.
4. Cut the cooled racks into individual ribs and place them in a large bowl. Add three-quarters of the honey-garlic glaze and toss to coat. Arrange the ribs, meaty side up on the prepared baking sheet and bake until they start to caramelize and sizzle, 10 to 12 minutes. Remove from the oven and brush with the remaining glaze.
5. Transfer the ribs to a serving platter and garnish with the sesame seeds and green onions.

SERVES 6 TO 8

Braised Ribs

2 racks pork baby back ribs
   (2 pounds/900 g each), cut in half
2 white onions, peeled and quartered
1 carrot, peeled and cut into 1-inch
   chunks
6 cloves garlic, crushed
¼ cup thinly sliced peeled fresh ginger
1 cup soy sauce

Honey-Garlic Glaze

¼ cup honey
2 tablespoons Orange Purée (page 236)
   or orange marmalade
2 tablespoons brown sugar
2 tablespoons soy sauce
2 tablespoons Hoisin Sauce (page 239 or
   store-bought)
1 teaspoon sambal oelek
½ teaspoon fish sauce
½ teaspoon minced garlic
½ teaspoon minced peeled fresh ginger

Garnishes

2 tablespoons toasted sesame seeds
1 bunch of green onions, thinly sliced on
   the diagonal

EAT WITH
Corn, Zucchini and Cheddar Sauté (page 162)
+
Honey Mustard Carrot Slaw (page 133)
+/or
Apple and Fennel Cabbage Slaw (page 133)

Maple-Bourbon Glazed Ham

Baked ham should not be reserved for only the holidays. This dish makes any meal a celebration. Here are the classic flavours of molasses and mustard with a splash of bourbon in a sticky, sweet glaze that caramelizes into a delectable crust—and also happens to fill the house with an intoxicating aroma.

Leftovers are great in sandwiches, quiche, eggs Benedict and fried rice.

1. Preheat the oven to 350°F.

MAKE THE MAPLE-BOURBON GLAZE

2. In a small saucepan, combine the ingredients. Bring to a boil over medium heat, stirring, and boil for about 1 minute. Remove from the heat.

BAKE THE HAM

3. Set the ham, cut side down, on a rack in a large roasting pan and pour in 2 cups of water. Trim the layer of fat to ½-inch thickness. Using a sharp knife, score the fat in a crosshatch pattern on the fatty side of the ham. Brush the ham with one-quarter of the maple-bourbon glaze and bake, basting every 20 minutes with the pan juices. Tent with foil if the ham is browning too quickly. Bake for 1½ to 2 hours until a meat thermometer or instant-read thermometer inserted into the thickest part of the ham (but not near the bone) registers 140°F. Spread the remaining glaze over the ham 10 minutes before you remove it from the oven. Allow the ham to rest for 10 minutes on a serving platter before slicing.

EAT WITH
Brussels Sprouts, Bacon and Toasted Fregola (page 157)
+
Buttery Mashed Potatoes (page 134)
+
Sweet Onion Cornbread (page 150)

SERVES 8 TO 10

1 cured smoked bone-in ham (8 to 10 pounds/3.5 to 4.5 kg)

Maple-Bourbon Glaze
½ cup maple syrup
½ cup bourbon or sweet apple cider
¼ cup packed brown sugar
¼ cup fancy molasses
2 tablespoons grated peeled fresh ginger
2 tablespoons Dijon mustard
2 tablespoons seedless tamarind paste
1 teaspoon red chili flakes
½ teaspoon cinnamon
½ teaspoon ground allspice

SIDES

Bacon and Egg Iceberg Salad with Avocado Dressing

This bacon and egg salad is deeply satisfying despite being simply a riff on a classic steakhouse iceberg salad. We like a lot goodies on our salads, and this one has so many—crispy bacon, "egg salad," sprouts, seasoned breadcrumbs and a lush green-goddessy avocado dressing.

MAKE THE AVOCADO DRESSING

1. Place the ingredients in a blender and blend until smooth. Season with salt and pepper. Store in an airtight container in the refrigerator for up to 1 week.

MAKE THE BACON AND EGG ICEBERG SALAD

2. Place the sliced lettuce on individual plates or a serving platter. Drizzle the avocado dressing over the lettuce and top with bacon, egg, sprouts, avocado, crispy panko breadcrumbs, chives and nutritional yeast, if using. Season with salt and pepper.

SERVES 4 TO 6

Avocado Dressing (makes 1½ cups)
1 avocado, pitted and peeled
½ cup mayonnaise
½ cup sour cream
3 tablespoons lemon juice
1 clove garlic, peeled
¼ cup loosely packed fresh flat-leaf parsley leaves
¼ cup loosely packed fresh dill
Kosher salt and freshly ground black pepper

Bacon and Egg Iceberg Salad
1 head iceberg lettuce, cut into 2-inch-thick horizontal slices
4 slices bacon, cooked crisp and crumbled
2 hard-boiled eggs, grated
1 cup sprouts (lentil, alfalfa, sunflower, broccoli or a combination)
1 avocado, pitted, peeled and diced
½ cup Crispy Panko Breadcrumbs (page 232)
¼ bunch of fresh chives, cut on the diagonal
2 tablespoons nutritional yeast (optional)
Kosher salt and freshly ground black pepper

Beet Salad with Horseradish Whipped Goat Cheese and Pistachio Granola

Beet and goat cheese salad became a popular menu item a few years back and is still going strong. No wonder, with its combination of the slightly sweet and acidic beets with the light, creamy cheese. Add in peppery greens, toasted nuts and lemony vinaigrette and you have a sumptuous crunchy delight that brightens any meal.

This is a version we make using local beets. We often use Chioggia (candy-stripe) and Cylindra beets, but we are also fans of Detroit Red Ace, Ruby Queen and Goldens, the common beets you find at the grocery store. Heading out to your local farmers' market will certainly offer you many choices to enjoy.

MAKE THE PISTACHIO GRANOLA

1. Preheat the oven to 325°F. Line a baking sheet with parchment paper.
2. In a large bowl, combine the oats and pistachios.
3. In a small saucepan, combine the canola oil, maple syrup, honey, salt, paprika and cayenne. Bring to a boil over medium heat, stirring constantly, then pour over the oat mixture and stir to combine.
4. Spread the granola on the prepared baking sheet and bake until crispy and toasted, about 20 minutes, stirring once halfway through the baking time. Let the granola cool to room temperature before storing in an airtight container for up to 2 weeks.

MAKE THE BEET SALAD WITH HORSERADISH WHIPPED GOAT CHEESE

5. Preheat the oven to 400°F.
6. Spread the salt in a large baking dish to create a bed for the beets. Place the beets on the salt and roast until fork-tender, about 45 minutes. Allow the beets to cool. Peel the beets and cut each one into 6 wedges.
7. In a food processor, combine the goat cheese, cream, horseradish, 1 tablespoon of the lemon juice and 1 teaspoon of the lemon zest. Pulse until completely combined. Scrape down the sides and give it a few more pulses. Season with salt and pepper.
8. In a medium bowl, whisk together the remaining lemon zest and juice, sherry vinegar, Dijon mustard, Worcestershire sauce and garlic. Gradually whisk in the canola oil and olive oil until emulsified. Season the vinaigrette with salt and pepper.
9. To serve, spread the horseradish goat cheese on a serving platter and arrange the beets on top. Toss the greens and golden beet with the vinaigrette and place on top of the beets. Garnish the salad with the sliced goat cheese and pistachio granola.

SERVES 4 TO 6

Pistachio Granola (makes about 1 cup)
½ cup instant/quick-cooking rolled oats
½ cup pistachios
2 tablespoons canola oil
2 tablespoons maple syrup
1 tablespoon honey
1 teaspoon kosher salt
½ teaspoon smoked paprika
¼ teaspoon cayenne pepper

Beet Salad with Horseradish Whipped Goat Cheese
1 cup kosher salt, more as needed (we use Diamond Crystal)
6 small (2-inch/5 cm diameter) red beets, scrubbed and trimmed
10 ounces (280 g) soft unripened goat cheese
¼ cup heavy (35%) cream
1 tablespoon grated fresh horseradish
Zest and juice of 1 lemon, divided
Freshly ground black pepper
2 tablespoons sherry vinegar
2 teaspoons Dijon mustard
1 teaspoon Worcestershire sauce
½ teaspoon minced garlic
⅓ cup canola oil
2 tablespoons olive oil
4 cups assorted greens (such as red oak, watercress, butter lettuce, spinach, arugula)
1 small golden beet, peeled and thinly sliced crosswise
1 log (4 ounces/125 g) ash-rind goat cheese (such as Le Cendrillon), cut into ½-inch slices

Caponata Salad with Pepper and Aubergine Relish

If you do not consider yourself a pepper or eggplant person, consider this dish the one that changes everything. Because everything in this chunky antipasto is nestled in together, heavily spiced and flavoured, you'll be amazed how the ingredients work together to form a greater whole that will impress you and your guests. It is the perfect accompaniment for pretty much everything: steak, rice and especially pita chips.

Our relish is named after our two daughters, Addie Pepper and Gemma Jet Aubergine. Pepper and Aubergine—you just have to love them!

1. Cut the eggplant crosswise into ½-inch slices and score both sides of each slice in a ½-inch diamond pattern. Season both sides of the eggplant with salt and pepper. In a large nonstick pan, heat 3 tablespoons of the olive oil over high heat. When the oil is very hot, working in batches, place the eggplant in the pan and cook until caramelized on the bottom, 2 to 3 minutes. Turn over and cook until caramelized on the other side, 1 to 2 minutes. Transfer the eggplant to a serving platter.

2. In the same pan, over medium heat, add the remaining 3 tablespoons olive oil. Add the red onion and cook, stirring occasionally, until translucent, 2 to 3 minutes. Stir in the olives, capers, garlic and sherry vinegar to make a vinaigrette. Remove from the heat and stir in the parsley. Season with salt and pepper.

3. Arrange the tomato slices, cherry tomatoes and lettuce on the platter with the eggplant. Drizzle the vinaigrette over the salad. Garnish with pepper and aubergine relish, goat cheese and basil leaves.

SERVES 4 TO 8

1 medium globe eggplant
Kosher salt and freshly ground black pepper
6 tablespoons olive oil, divided
1 red onion, diced
¼ cup pitted Kalamata olives, roughly chopped
2 tablespoons drained capers, roughly chopped
1 clove garlic, minced
3 tablespoons sherry vinegar
⅓ cup fresh flat-leaf parsley leaves, roughly chopped
2 heirloom tomatoes, sliced
1 cup cherry tomatoes, cut in half
1 head butter lettuce, leaves separated

Garnishes
Pepper and Aubergine Relish (page 243)
½ cup crumbled goat cheese
Fresh basil leaves

Castelfranco Radicchio, Orange and Burrata Salad with Walnut Date Vinaigrette

If you have never eaten Castelfranco radicchio, get ready to fall in love. This slightly bitter green from Italy is sturdy enough to play well with the spirited oranges and dates. Burrata is the star in this dish—a bright, shiny star. All the ingredients work perfectly together.

Make sure you pull the burrata from the refrigerator a good hour or so before you serve so that it's at room temperature and at its best—creamy and ready to shine.

1. In a small bowl, whisk together the olive oil, walnut oil, orange juice, sherry vinegar and shallots until emulsified. Season with salt and pepper.
2. Place the orange segments and dates in a large bowl. Toss with 2 table-spoons of the vinaigrette and let marinate for a few minutes. Add the radicchio, lettuce, arugula, parsley and mint. Gently toss with enough additional vinaigrette to dress the greens. Season with salt and pepper.
3. To serve, arrange the salad on a serving platter. Tear the burrata into pieces using your hands and arrange on top of the salad. Drizzle any remaining vinaigrette over the burrata and around the salad. Garnish with the toasted walnuts and season with salt and pepper.

SERVES 4 TO 6

½ cup olive oil
2 tablespoons walnut oil
⅓ cup orange juice
3 tablespoons sherry vinegar
1 tablespoon finely diced shallots
Kosher salt and freshly ground black pepper
4 oranges, segmented, juice reserved
½ cup pitted Medjool dates, thinly sliced
1 head Castelfranco radicchio, leaves separated
1 head Boston lettuce, leaves separated
1 cup packed baby arugula
½ cup packed fresh flat-leaf parsley leaves
¼ cup fresh mint, leaves torn
8 ounces (225 g) burrata cheese
½ cup toasted chopped walnuts

Endive and Apple Salad with Marcona Almonds and Ginger Miso Dressing

The ultimate salad is at home at any meal, any time, any day. This is one of those salads. It impeccably balances sweet (apples) and bitter (endive) flavours with creamy (dressing) and crunchy (almonds) textures.

Though you can use regular almonds here, we recommend looking for the sweeter, softer, juicier Marcona variety. One bite and you will see why we eat them by the handful.

1. In a large salad bowl, combine the endives, apples and dill.
2. In a small bowl, combine the mayonnaise, sour cream, lemon juice, rice vinegar, miso and ginger. Whisk together well. Season with salt and pepper.
3. Add the dressing to the salad and gently toss to mix. Serve in the salad bowl or on individual plates. Garnish with the almonds and sprinkle with the nutritional yeast.

SERVES 4 TO 6

6 Belgian endives, cored and thinly sliced lengthwise
2 Gala apples or your favourite variety, cored and thinly sliced
¼ cup chopped fresh dill
½ cup mayonnaise
¼ cup sour cream
1 tablespoon lemon juice
1 tablespoon seasoned rice vinegar
2 teaspoons white miso
2 teaspoons finely grated peeled fresh ginger
Kosher salt and freshly ground black pepper
½ cup Marcona almonds, toasted and coarsely chopped
2 tablespoons nutritional yeast

Fattoush Salad with Heirloom Tomatoes and Za'atar Pita Crisps

Fattoush salad quenches that desire for a sandwich while being miles from yet another dreary lunch. Explosive herbs tumbled together with za'atar-dusted pita chips, ripe heirloom tomato and red onion, along with a hearty dose of feta, makes for a beautiful side dish, but it is also a deeply satisfying meal on its own.

1. Preheat the oven to 350°F. Line a baking sheet with parchment paper.
2. In a small bowl, stir together ¼ cup of the olive oil, thyme, sumac and 2 teaspoons of the za'atar spice.
3. Spread the torn pita on the prepared baking sheet. Drizzle with the za'atar oil mixture, season with salt and pepper, and toss until evenly coated. Bake until golden and crisp, 12 to 15 minutes. Let cool on the baking sheet.
4. In a large bowl, whisk together the lemon juice, honey, remaining ¼ cup olive oil and remaining 2 teaspoons za'atar spice. Add the tomatoes, red onion, cucumber, mint, dill, parsley and pita crisps and toss to coat. Season with salt and pepper.
5. Transfer the salad to a serving platter. Top with the feta, microgreens and edible flowers.

SERVES 4 TO 6

½ cup olive oil, divided
1 tablespoon finely chopped fresh thyme leaves
½ teaspoon sumac
4 teaspoons Za'atar Spice (page 230 or store-bought), divided
3 (6-inch/15 cm) pita breads, cut in half crosswise and torn into 1-inch pieces
Kosher salt and freshly ground black pepper
3 tablespoons lemon juice
2 teaspoons honey
2 pounds (900 g) heirloom tomatoes, sliced
1 small red onion, thinly sliced
2 to 3 mini cucumbers, cut into ribbons
½ cup loosely packed torn fresh mint leaves
½ cup roughly chopped fresh dill
½ cup loosely packed torn fresh flat-leaf parsley leaves
4 ounces (115 g) feta cheese, crumbled
Microgreens and edible flowers, for garnish

Warm Lentil Mirepoix Salad with Goat Cheese and Almonds

Mirepoix—the mixture of lightly cooked carrot, onion and celery—is a basic culinary ingredient that adds extra dimension to a dish. It is why soups, stews, casseroles, braised meats and marinades taste so good. It does not take long to make a divine dish when you combine mirepoix with lentils, a staple in French cookery. Puy lentils have a delicious rustic nutty flavour and they hold their shape really well in this warm salad topped with tangy goat cheese and toasty almonds.

Grown in the volcanic soil of the Puy region in France, Puy lentils are known for their dark slate colour and rich, peppery flavour.

1. In a medium saucepan, combine the lentils and thyme with plenty of lightly salted water to cover the lentils. Bring to a boil over high heat, then reduce the heat and simmer until the lentils are tender but not mushy, 15 to 20 minutes.

2. While the lentils are cooking, add the butter, carrots, onion and celery to a large skillet. Cook over medium heat, stirring frequently, until the vegetables are tender, 5 to 10 minutes.

3. In a small bowl, whisk together the shallot, red wine vinegar, mustard and olive oil until emulsified. Season with salt and pepper.

4. Drain the lentils well, discard the thyme sprigs, and transfer the lentils to the skillet of vegetables. Drizzle with the dressing and toss to evenly coat. Fold in the parsley and almonds.

5. Serve the salad warm or at room temperature. If served warm, crumble the goat cheese on top at the last minute so it does not melt but just softens slightly. The salad can be made up to 2 days ahead and stored, covered and refrigerated.

SERVES 4 TO 6

1½ cups Puy or other green lentils, drained and rinsed
2 sprigs fresh thyme
3 tablespoons unsalted butter
1 cup finely diced peeled carrots
1 cup finely diced white onion
1 cup finely diced celery
1 small shallot, minced
3 tablespoons red wine vinegar
1 tablespoon Dijon mustard
⅓ cup olive oil
Kosher salt and freshly ground black pepper
½ cup finely chopped fresh flat-leaf parsley
½ cup almonds, toasted and coarsely chopped
¾ cup crumbled goat or feta cheese

Lobster Potato Salad

We have so many wonderful memories of our adventures exploring Prince Edward Island, one of the most beautiful places we have visited. We are grateful to have met so many amazing people who live there and who always made us feel like we were at home with family.

This luscious lobster salad is all about the succulent, tender lobster meat, lots of lemony dressing and lots of fresh dill. Better yet, this East Coast classic is so easy to prepare at home.

1. Prepare a very large ice bath.
2. Bring a large pot of salted water to a boil. When the water is boiling, add the lobsters and boil until they turn bright red, about 12 minutes. Drain well and transfer the lobsters to the ice bath to cool. Drain again. Twist the bodies from the lobster tails. Using kitchen scissors, cut along the underside of the shells and remove the meat. Crack the claws and knuckles and remove the meat. Cut the lobster meat into chunks and transfer to a large bowl.
3. Bring a large pot of salted water to a boil. Add the potatoes and cook until fork-tender, about 15 minutes. Remove the potatoes with a slotted spoon and transfer to a large bowl to cool.
4. In the same pot of boiling water, cook the green beans for 2 minutes, until bright green and crisp. Add the sea asparagus, if using, and cook for 30 seconds. Drain the vegetables and transfer to a bowl of ice water. Let stand for 5 minutes, then drain well.
5. Cut the cooled potatoes into ¼-inch slices.
6. In a medium bowl, whisk together the lemon juice, sherry vinegar, capers, dill, shallot and mustard. Slowly whisk in the olive oil until emulsified. Season with salt and pepper.
7. Toss the lettuce leaves with a few tablespoons of the dressing and arrange on a serving platter.
8. In a large bowl, toss the potatoes, green beans and sea asparagus with half of the dressing. Spoon the potato salad over the lettuce leaves. Top with the lobster and drizzle with the remaining dressing. Garnish with the potato chips and serve with lemon caper rémoulade on the side.

SERVES 4 TO 6

2 live lobsters (1¼ pounds/565 g each)
1 pound (450 g) small purple or fingerling potatoes
8 ounces (225 g) green beans, trimmed
2 ounces (57 g) sea asparagus (optional)
2 tablespoons lemon juice
1 tablespoon sherry vinegar
2 tablespoons chopped drained capers
2 tablespoons chopped fresh dill
1 tablespoon finely diced shallot
2 teaspoons Dijon mustard
¼ cup olive oil
Kosher salt and freshly ground black pepper
2 heads butter lettuce, leaves separated
Potato chips, for garnish
Lemon Caper Rémoulade (page 245)

Lyonnaise Salad with Brown Butter Parmesan Croutons

This salad can catapult you to another place and time. This French bistro salad has the perfect balance of frisée lettuce, thick-cut pieces of bacon and warm mustardy vinaigrette, all deliciously topped with a poached egg. This is the salad to enjoy while imagining yourself sitting at a café on the sunny banks of the Seine.

MAKE THE BROWN BUTTER PARMESAN CROUTONS

1. Preheat the oven to 375°F. Line a small baking sheet with parchment paper.
2. Place the cubed bread in a large bowl.
3. Melt the butter in a medium saucepan over medium-low heat. Add the garlic and cook, swirling often, until the foaming subsides, the butter has turned golden brown and the garlic is fragrant, 6 to 8 minutes. Drizzle the garlic butter over the bread and toss with the Parmesan to coat. Season with salt and pepper.
4. Spread out the bread cubes on the prepared baking sheet. Bake until the croutons are deep golden brown and crisp, 20 to 25 minutes. Let cool on the baking sheet. Use immediately or store in an airtight container at room temperature for up to 1 week.

MAKE THE LYONNAISE SALAD

5. In a large skillet over medium heat, cook the bacon, stirring often, until crisp, 5 to 6 minutes. Using a slotted spoon, transfer the bacon to a plate lined with paper towel to drain.
6. Drain all but ¼ cup of bacon fat from the pan. Reduce the heat to low. Add the garlic and shallots and cook until softened, 1 to 2 minutes. Remove the skillet from the heat. Whisk in the mustard and 2 tablespoons of the white wine vinegar. While whisking, slowly drizzle in the olive oil until emulsified. Add the lemon zest and juice. Season with salt and pepper.
7. In a large bowl, toss the frisée and red oak lettuce with the warm vinaigrette. Transfer to a large shallow serving bowl.
8. Bring a 4-quart saucepan of water to a boil. When the water is boiling, add the remaining 1 tablespoon white wine vinegar, then reduce the heat to a simmer. Using a slotted spoon, swirl the water. One at a time, crack an egg into a ramekin, then slide the egg into the water; cook until the egg whites are set, about 2 minutes. Using a slotted spoon, blot the eggs on paper towel to remove excess water, then place them on top of the salad. Garnish with the brown butter Parmesan croutons and the bacon.

SERVES 4 TO 6

Brown Butter Parmesan Croutons (makes about 2 cups)

2 cups cubed sourdough or multigrain bread
½ cup unsalted butter
4 cloves garlic, smashed
¼ cup grated Parmesan cheese
Kosher salt and freshly ground black pepper

Lyonnaise Salad

4 slices thick-cut bacon, cut into ¼-inch dice
2 cloves garlic, minced
2 shallots, finely diced
2 teaspoons Dijon mustard
3 tablespoons white wine vinegar, divided
3 tablespoons olive oil
Zest and juice of ½ lemon
Kosher salt and freshly ground black pepper
2 heads frisée lettuce, cut into bite-size pieces
1 head red oak or romaine lettuce, roughly chopped
4 to 6 eggs

Romaine and Treviso Salad with Pancetta Vinaigrette and Caesar Aioli

This is our version of a Caesar salad. Baby gem lettuce delivers a crisp bite tossed with Treviso radicchio, a stunning purple, pointed, slightly bitter lettuce that is milder than the common round radicchio. These wonderful greens are topped with a warm herb vinaigrette replete with crispy salt-cured pork belly, sweet plump golden raisins and pine nuts, all accompanied by a zippy Caesar aioli. It is a sensational first course that can be a hard act to follow.

MAKE THE CAESAR AIOLI

1. In a medium bowl, whisk together the egg yolks, lemon zest, lemon juice and mustard. Whisking constantly, drizzle in the canola oil and olive oil until emulsified.
2. Whisk in the garlic, chives and capers. Season well with salt and pepper. Use immediately or store in an airtight container in the refrigerator for up to 2 weeks. The Caesar aioli is a great condiment for sandwiches, grilled meats or fish.

MAKE THE PANCETTA VINAIGRETTE

3. In a medium saucepan over low heat, stir the pancetta until some of the fat begins to render. Increase the heat to medium and cook the pancetta, stirring frequently, until crispy, about 5 minutes. Using a slotted spoon, transfer the crispy pancetta to a plate lined with paper towel to drain. Keep the fat in the pan.
4. Return the pan to medium heat. Add the garlic and shallot, swirl, and immediately stir in the white wine vinegar, olive oil, maple syrup and mustard. Bring the mixture to a boil and cook for 1 minute. Remove from the heat and add the raisins, pine nuts, and lemon zest and juice. Taste and season with salt and pepper. Stir in the crispy pancetta.

ASSEMBLE THE ROMAINE AND TREVISO SALAD

5. Spread about ½ cup of the Caesar aioli over a serving platter. Arrange the romaine, Baby gem, radicchio and herbs on top. Spoon the warm pancetta vinaigrette over the greens, reserving any remaining vinaigrette to serve on the side. Garnish the salad with the Parmesan.

SERVES 4 TO 6

Caesar Aioli (makes 1½ cups)
2 large egg yolks
1 teaspoon lemon zest
2 tablespoons lemon juice
1 teaspoon Dijon mustard
¾ cup canola oil
½ cup olive oil
1 clove garlic, minced
2 tablespoons chopped fresh chives
1 tablespoon chopped drained capers
Kosher salt and freshly ground black pepper

Pancetta Vinaigrette
4 ounces (115 g) pancetta (or 5 slices thick-cut bacon), cut into ⅛-inch cubes
3 cloves garlic, minced
1 shallot, minced
¼ cup white wine vinegar
¼ cup extra-virgin olive oil
3 tablespoons maple syrup
3 tablespoons Dijon mustard
¼ cup golden raisins
¼ cup toasted pine nuts
Zest and juice of ½ lemon
Kosher salt and freshly ground black pepper

Romaine and Treviso Salad
2 romaine hearts, quartered lengthwise
2 Baby gem lettuce, leaves torn apart
2 Treviso radicchio, cut in half lengthwise
1 cup mixed fresh herb leaves (such as parsley, basil and dill)

¼ cup shaved Parmesan cheese, for serving

Honey Mustard Carrot Slaw

This creamy carrot slaw is fresh and full of flavour. A perfect side for barbecue days full of burgers, ribs and cold beer.

1. In a large bowl, combine the mayonnaise, sour cream, honey, mustard, apple cider vinegar, celery seeds, and lemon zest and juice. Whisk together well. Add the carrots, chives and parsley and toss together well. Season with salt and pepper.

SERVES 4 TO 6

¼ cup mayonnaise
¼ cup sour cream
2 tablespoons honey
2 tablespoons grainy mustard
1 tablespoon apple cider vinegar
½ teaspoon celery seeds
1 tablespoon lemon zest
2 tablespoons lemon juice
4 carrots, peeled and grated
2 tablespoons chopped fresh chives
1 tablespoon chopped fresh flat-leaf parsley
Kosher salt and freshly ground black pepper

Apple and Fennel Cabbage Slaw

This apple and fennel slaw is crisp and refreshing. A perfect side for our sticky Honey-Garlic Ribs (page 107) and a glass of chilled rosé.

1. In a small bowl, combine the apple cider vinegar, lemon juice, sugar and ground fennel. Slowly whisk in the olive oil until emulsified. Season with salt and pepper.
2. In a large bowl, toss together the apple, fennel, cabbage and dill. Pour the dressing over the slaw and mix together.

SERVES 4 TO 6

¼ cup apple cider vinegar
¼ cup lemon juice
1 tablespoon granulated sugar
1 teaspoon ground fennel seeds
¼ cup olive oil
Kosher salt and freshly ground black pepper
1 apple, cored and julienned
1 fennel bulb, thinly sliced horizontally
½ green cabbage, thinly sliced
¼ cup chopped fresh dill

Buttery Mashed Potatoes

Every family needs a stellar mashed potato recipe. This has been our go-to for decades. It is absolutely foolproof. The only requirement is using fresh Yukon Gold potatoes, cooking them until fork-tender, then adding milk and lots of butter to make them rich and delicious.

The fresher your potatoes, the better the results. Look for slightly damp skin and a fresh, earthy scent.

1. Rinse the potatoes under cold running water, then place them in a pot of salted cold water. Bring to a simmer and cook until very tender, 20 to 25 minutes. Drain the potatoes.
2. In the same pot, bring the milk and 8 tablespoons of the butter to a simmer until the butter has melted. Remove from the heat. Pass the hot potatoes through a ricer or food mill into the hot milk mixture and stir gently to combine (or mash in the pot with the milk and butter). Season with salt and pepper. Serve in a bowl, topped with the remaining 2 tablespoons butter.

SERVES 4

2 pounds (900 g) Yukon Gold potatoes, peeled and quartered
¾ cup whole milk
8 tablespoons (1 stick) + 2 tablespoons unsalted butter, softened, divided
Kosher salt and freshly ground black pepper

Baked Sweet Potatoes with Chipotle Lime Crema, Bacon, Pecans and Rosemary Honey

These triple-loaded baked sweet potatoes topped with a cornucopia of exquisite Mexican-inspired chipotle-lime cream and pecans are sure to be a hit at the dinner table. Quick and easy to prepare, these dressed-up potatoes are packed with lots of flavour and texture.

We recommend buying Garnet or Jewel sweet potatoes. These varieties, which have sweet orange flesh and a brownish-orange skin, are the best for baking.

BAKE THE SWEET POTATOES

1. Position a rack in the middle of the oven. Place a foil-lined baking sheet on the lower rack to catch any oil drips. Preheat the oven to 450°F.
2. Using a fork or paring knife, puncture each potato in several spots. Microwave the potatoes on high for 5 minutes. Rub each potato with a light coat of olive oil. Arrange the sweet potatoes directly on the middle oven rack. Bake until a fork can be easily inserted into the centre of each potato, 30 to 40 minutes.
3. When the potatoes are almost done, cook the bacon in a large skillet over medium-high heat until just about crisp, 2 to 3 minutes.

MAKE THE CHIPOTLE LIME CREMA

4. In a small bowl, stir together the ingredients. Season with salt and pepper. Refrigerate until ready to use.

TO FINISH

5. Slice the cooked sweet potatoes open lengthwise and scoop the flesh into a medium bowl. Add the butter and season with salt and pepper. Roughly mash the sweet potatoes just until the butter is incorporated.
6. Scoop the mashed potato back into skins. Top with the bacon, chipotle lime crema and toasted pecans and drizzle with the rosemary honey.

SERVES 4 TO 6

Baked Sweet Potatoes
4 to 6 large sweet potatoes
3 tablespoons olive oil
4 to 6 slices thick-cut bacon, diced
4 tablespoons unsalted butter, at room temperature
Kosher salt and freshly ground black pepper
½ cup toasted pecans

Chipotle Lime Crema
½ cup sour cream
Zest and juice of 1 lime
½ teaspoon chipotle chili powder
¼ teaspoon garlic powder
Kosher salt and freshly ground black pepper

Rosemary Honey (page 235), for serving

Crispy Smashed Potatoes with Caramelized Onion Dip

Our homemade French onion dip is the best, and a fun play on chips and dip. All those caramelized onions in a savoury herb sour cream dip are the most delicious accompaniment to these hot, golden, crispy potatoes.

SERVES 4 TO 6

PREPARE THE POTATOES

1. Place the potatoes in a medium saucepan and cover with 2 inches of water. Season generously with salt and bring to a boil over medium-high heat. Reduce the heat and simmer until the potatoes are tender when pierced with a knife, 20 to 25 minutes. Drain and set aside until cool enough to handle.

MEANWHILE, MAKE THE CARAMELIZED ONION DIP

2. While the potatoes are cooking, in a medium saucepan, heat the olive oil over medium heat. Add the onions and cook, stirring occasionally, until they are caramelized, about 20 minutes. Remove from the heat and let cool.
3. In a medium bowl, combine the cooled onions, sour cream, half of the chives, the parsley and lemon zest. Mix together until smooth. Season with salt and pepper. Transfer to a small serving dish and garnish with the remaining chives.

BAKE THE SMASHED POTATOES

4. Preheat the oven to 375°F. Line a baking sheet with parchment paper.
5. Place the potatoes on the prepared baking sheet. Using a large fork or the heel of your hand, gently squish them. Be careful to keep them in one piece.
6. In a small saucepan, melt the butter with the olive oil, thyme and rosemary. Season with salt and pepper. Drizzle the potatoes with the seasoned butter. Bake for 20 minutes or until deep golden and crispy. Turn the potatoes and cook on the other side until crisp and golden, 10 to 15 minutes.
7. Transfer the potatoes to a serving platter and season lightly with salt and pepper. Serve with the caramelized onion dip.

Crispy Smashed Potatoes

2 pounds (900 g) small Yukon Gold or fingerling potatoes, scrubbed
⅓ cup unsalted butter
2 tablespoons olive oil
3 sprigs fresh thyme, cut into 2-inch pieces
1 sprig fresh rosemary, cut into 2-inch pieces
Kosher salt and freshly ground black pepper

Caramelized Onion Dip

1 tablespoon olive oil
2 white onions, thinly sliced
2 cups sour cream
2 tablespoons chopped fresh chives, divided
1 tablespoon chopped fresh flat-leaf parsley
Zest of 1 lemon
Kosher salt and freshly ground black pepper

Basmati Rice with Spiced Tomato Chutney

Steamed rice is a useful side but can become a bit ho-hum if relied on too heavily. That is why we have amped things up with a rich infusion of tomato and fennel and the powerful scent of cardamom.

We recommend buying whole cardamom pods rather than ground. Green pods are the most common. They impart warm lemony notes to dishes. The pod of the black variety imparts a slight smoky flavour. Cardamom is one of the world's very ancient spices that is so aromatic and quite magical.

MAKE THE SPICED TOMATO CHUTNEY

1. Heat a large skillet over high heat. Add the olive oil and cherry tomatoes and cook, stirring occasionally, until the tomatoes start to blister, about 2 minutes. Stir in the garlic and cook until it starts to caramelize, about 1 minute.
2. Add the star anise, cinnamon stick, chili powder, cayenne, cumin, sugar and thyme and continue cooking, stirring frequently, until the sugar dissolves, about 2 minutes. Stir in the rice vinegar and grated tomato and simmer over low heat until the mixture thickens, 6 to 8 minutes. Remove from the heat. Remove and discard the cinnamon stick, star anise and thyme sprig. Season well with salt and pepper. Let cool. Store in an airtight container in the refrigerator for up to 2 weeks.

MAKE THE BASMATI RICE

3. Wash the rice under cold running water until it runs clear.
4. Heat the vegetable oil in a medium saucepan over medium-high heat. Stir in the coriander, cumin and fennel seeds, cardamom pods, cinnamon stick and star anise, and heat until the spices splutter, about 30 seconds. Add the lime leaves and fry for a few seconds. Add the tomato paste and cook, stirring frequently, for 2 minutes. Add the boiling water and the salt, stir well, then stir in the drained rice. Bring to a boil, then reduce the heat to low, cover and cook for 15 minutes. Remove from the heat, keep covered, and let stand for 5 minutes. Fluff the rice with a fork.
5. Serve the hot rice and the spiced tomato chutney separately.

SERVES 4 TO 6

Spiced Tomato Chutney (makes about 1½ cups)
2 tablespoons olive oil
1 cup cherry tomatoes, cut in half
3 cloves garlic, thinly sliced
1 star anise
1 cinnamon stick
¼ teaspoon chili powder
⅛ teaspoon cayenne pepper
⅛ teaspoon ground cumin
2 tablespoons granulated sugar
1 sprig fresh thyme
1 tablespoon unseasoned rice vinegar
1 beefsteak tomato, grated (about 1 cup)
Kosher salt and freshly ground black pepper

Basmati Rice
2 cups basmati rice
2 tablespoons vegetable oil
1 teaspoon coriander seeds
1 teaspoon cumin seeds
1 teaspoon fennel seeds
4 green cardamom pods
1 cinnamon stick
1 star anise
2 kaffir lime leaves
2 teaspoons tomato paste
3 cups boiling water
2 teaspoons kosher salt

Shrimp and Egg Fried Rice

A few things we have learned about making incredibly delicious shrimp and egg fried rice are worth sharing. Use leftover rice, use lots of shrimp and listen to chef Carl, a long-time friend and colleague at our restaurant. He gave us the perfect recipe for seasoning the fried rice with maple syrup, sesame oil and soy sauce.

1. Season the eggs with salt and pepper. In a very large skillet or wok, heat 2 tablespoons of the canola oil over high heat. When the oil is very hot, pour the eggs into the skillet and scramble until just cooked through, about 1 minute. Transfer to a plate.
2. Heat the remaining 2 tablespoons canola oil in the skillet over high heat. Add the garlic and ginger and stir-fry for 1 minute. Add the soy sauce, sesame oil and maple syrup and cook for about 30 seconds. Add the cooked rice, shrimp, peas and reserved eggs. Season with salt and stir-fry until the rice is hot, about 2 minutes. Transfer to a serving bowl and sprinkle with the green onions.

SERVES 4 TO 6

4 large eggs, beaten
Kosher salt and freshly ground black
  pepper
4 tablespoons canola oil, divided
1 tablespoon minced garlic
2 tablespoons minced peeled fresh ginger
¼ cup soy sauce
2 tablespoons sesame oil
2 teaspoons maple syrup
6 cups cooked long-grain rice, cooled
1½ cups peeled and deveined cooked
  salad or cocktail shrimp
1 cup thawed frozen peas
4 green onions, thinly sliced

Mushroom Risotto

The keys to a good risotto are using the correct ratio of liquid to rice, tending to it frequently and infusing the rice with strong, earthy flavours. In addition to a medley of fresh mushrooms browned in butter until nutty, and our super-hero Mushroom Powder, we add caramelized shallots, sprigs of thyme and a heavy dose of Parmesan and chopped parsley for a truly sophisticated dish that can be enjoyed at the dinner table or on the couch in matching onesies.

White or button mushrooms (also called table or champignon) are fine in this recipe, but the more diverse your mushroom selection, the more depth your dish will yield. So grab some chanterelles, cremini, oysters, porcini, portobellos and shiitakes, and toast to mushroom madness!

SERVES 4 TO 6

4 cups low-sodium chicken or Vegetable Stock (page 238 or store-bought)
4 tablespoons unsalted butter, divided
2 tablespoons olive oil
1 pound (450 g) assorted mushrooms (such as shiitake, oyster, beech, chanterelle and cremini), cut into 1-inch pieces
Kosher salt and freshly ground black pepper
2 cloves garlic, minced
2 sprigs fresh thyme
¼ cup finely diced shallots
1½ cups arborio rice
½ cup dry white wine (optional)
½ cup grated Parmesan cheese, more for serving
¼ cup packed fresh flat-leaf parsley leaves, chopped
1 tablespoon Mushroom Powder (page 235)

1. In a medium saucepan, bring the chicken stock to a simmer.
2. In a large saucepan, melt 2 tablespoons of the butter with the olive oil over medium-high heat. Add the mushrooms and cook, stirring occasionally, until golden brown, 3 to 4 minutes. Season with salt and pepper. Transfer the mushrooms to a medium bowl.
3. Return the saucepan to medium heat. Add the remaining 2 tablespoons butter, the garlic, thyme sprigs and shallots and cook, stirring, until the shallots are caramelized, about 2 minutes. Add the rice and stir for 1 minute.
4. Add the white wine, if using, and simmer for 2 minutes, until mostly evaporated.
5. Add 2 cups of simmering stock and cook, stirring frequently, until the stock has almost completely absorbed, 3 to 4 minutes, before adding another ½ cup stock. Repeat, adding ½ cup stock at a time, until all the stock is absorbed. The rice should be creamy but just firm. Stir in half of the mushrooms, the Parmesan, parsley and mushroom powder. Season with salt and pepper. Remove from the heat and keep warm.
6. Reheat the remaining mushrooms in a small skillet over medium-high heat. Spoon the risotto into a serving bowl and top with the mushrooms.

Moroccan Couscous

This couscous is quite complex in flavour but it is simple to make. It is a hearty dish, packed with sun-dried tomatoes, golden raisins, chickpeas, mint, dill and toasted almonds. Couscous infused with ras el hanout spice, with its blend of cinnamon, ginger and cumin, is the perfect base to carry all those bountiful flavours.

1. In a medium saucepan, combine the chicken stock, butter, ras el hanout and salt and bring to a boil. Stir in the couscous, cover tightly with a lid and remove from the heat. Let the couscous steam for 5 minutes. Use a fork to fluff the couscous and break up any clumps. Keep warm.

2. In a large skillet over medium-high heat, combine the olive oil, onion and garlic and cook, stirring frequently, until the onions are softened and caramelized, 3 to 4 minutes. Stir in the sun-dried tomatoes, raisins and chickpeas and cook for 2 minutes until hot. Add the lemon zest and juice, and season well with salt and pepper.

3. Transfer the couscous to a large serving bowl, then fluff the couscous with a fork to separate the grains. Add the chickpea mixture, parsley and dill and toss to combine. Season with salt and pepper. Garnish with the almonds and mint.

SERVES 4 TO 6

1¾ cups Roasted Chicken Stock (page 237 or store-bought) or water
2 tablespoons unsalted butter
2 teaspoons Ras el Hanout Spice (page 230 or store-bought)
½ teaspoon kosher salt
1½ cups couscous
2 tablespoons olive oil
1 white onion, thinly sliced
2 cloves garlic, minced
¼ cup sun-dried tomatoes, sliced
¼ cup golden raisins
1 can (19 ounces/540 mL) chickpeas, drained and rinsed
1 teaspoon lemon zest
2 tablespoons lemon juice
Kosher salt and freshly ground black pepper
¼ cup packed fresh flat-leaf parsley leaves, chopped
¼ cup packed fresh dill, chopped
½ cup toasted slivered almonds
2 tablespoons chopped fresh mint

Cheesy Garlic Pull-Apart Bread

There's just something so good about the combination of bread, butter, tons of cheese and garlic. Instead of a regular old baguette garlic bread, we add an interactive component and make this a fun bread that you pull right out of the pan.

In addition to its amazing cheesiness, what is great about this dish is that you can put it in the oven, set a timer and forget about it. Just let it do its thing and take credit for the wondrous results.

1. Preheat the oven to 375°F. Butter a 13 x 9-inch baking pan.
2. In a small bowl, combine the sugar, yeast and milk. Cover and let sit for about 10 minutes or until the mixture is frothy.
3. Sift the flour into a large bowl. Add the salt, then rub 4 tablespoons of the butter into the flour to a coarse meal consistency. Stir in the yeast mixture, egg, confit garlic and cheddar cheese and stir until a soft, sticky dough forms. Turn out the dough onto a lightly floured surface and knead until smooth.
4. Divide the dough into 20 pieces. Roll each piece into a ball. Place in the prepared baking pan. Cover with a kitchen towel and let stand at room temperature for 30 minutes or until doubled in size.
5. In a small saucepan, melt the remaining 1 tablespoon butter. Brush the melted butter over the buns and sprinkle with the Parmesan. Bake until golden brown, 25 to 30 minutes. Allow to cool slightly and serve in the pan or turn out onto a platter.

MAKES 20 BUNS

¼ cup granulated sugar

2 tablespoons active dry yeast

1½ cups whole or 2% milk, warm

4 cups all-purpose flour

1 teaspoon kosher salt

5 tablespoons unsalted butter, divided

1 egg, lightly beaten

1 tablespoon Confit Garlic (page 233) or
(1 clove garlic, chopped)

2 cups grated aged cheddar cheese

¼ cup grated Parmesan cheese

Sweet Onion Cornbread

Caramelizing Vidalia onions intensifies their beautiful natural sweetness and adds depth to this soft, crumbly cornbread finished with a golden crust. This is a warm and comforting side perfect for any night of the week, but a great addition to a brunch table, too.

MAKE THE CARAMELIZED ONIONS

1. Preheat the oven to 350°F.
2. Heat the canola oil in a 10-inch cast-iron skillet over medium-high heat. Add the onions and cook, without stirring, until golden brown on the bottom, 2 to 3 minutes. Reduce the heat to medium, add the butter and sugar, and toss to coat. Cook, stirring occasionally, until onions have softened, about 2 minutes. Add the sherry vinegar, season with salt and pepper, and continue to cook and stir until the vinegar evaporates, 1 to 2 minutes. Remove from the heat. Spread the onions evenly in the pan.

MAKE THE CORNBREAD

3. In a large bowl, stir together the flour, cornmeal, sugar, baking powder and salt.
4. In a medium bowl, whisk together the eggs, milk, canola oil, butter and corn kernels. Stir the egg mixture into the flour mixture until just combined. Pour the batter over the onions in the skillet. Bake until golden brown, 35 to 45 minutes. Let cool in the skillet on a wire rack for at least 15 minutes.
5. Run a knife around the edge of the pan to loosen the cornbread. Place a cutting board over the pan and turn the pan over to release the cornbread onto the board. The cornbread can be stored in an airtight container in the refrigerator for up to 2 days.

SERVES 8 TO 10

Caramelized Onions

1 tablespoon canola oil

1 large sweet onion, preferably Vidalia (about 8 ounces/225 g), sliced

2 teaspoons unsalted butter

1 tablespoon granulated sugar

2 tablespoons sherry vinegar or balsamic vinegar

Kosher salt and freshly ground black pepper

Cornbread

2 cups all-purpose flour

1 cup cornmeal

¾ cup granulated sugar

1 tablespoon baking powder

½ teaspoon kosher salt

2 large eggs

1½ cups whole or 2% milk

1¼ cups canola oil

4 tablespoons unsalted butter, melted

1 cup fresh or thawed frozen sweet corn kernels

Asparagus with Citrus, Anchovy and Almond Butter

After a very long winter, we always wait in anticipation for the first signs of spring when our farmers' market starts to fill up with bright green pencil-sized stalks of locally grown asparagus. It really does not matter if we sauté asparagus in a pan or char it on the grill, it will always be one of our ultimate favourite vegetables. We try to enjoy asparagus as much as we can when it's in season.

Cook only as much asparagus as you need for one meal, since it usually does not make for great leftovers. For the freshest flavour, try to eat asparagus the same day you buy it.

1. Cut the peel and white pith from the orange. Cut along the sides of the membranes to release the segments into a small bowl. Squeeze the juice from the membranes into the bowl. Set aside.

2. Heat a large skillet over medium heat. Add 2 tablespoons of the olive oil and the asparagus and cook, turning occasionally, until crisp-tender, 3 to 5 minutes. Season with salt and pepper. Transfer the asparagus to a serving platter.

3. To make the sauce, in the same skillet, over medium heat, heat the remaining 1 tablespoon olive oil. Add the anchovies, garlic and shallot and cook, stirring occasionally, for 1 to 2 minutes, allowing the anchovies to break up. Add the orange segments and juices and lemon zest and juice; cook for another 30 seconds. Add the butter, almond butter and parsley and stir together. Season with salt and pepper. When the butter has melted into the sauce, spoon the sauce over the asparagus. Garnish with the toasted almonds.

SERVES 4 TO 6

1 orange
3 tablespoons olive oil, divided
1½ pounds (675 g) fresh asparagus, tough ends trimmed
Kosher salt and freshly ground black pepper
2 oil-packed anchovy fillets
2 cloves garlic, minced
1 shallot, finely diced
1 teaspoon lemon zest
1 tablespoon lemon juice
2 tablespoons unsalted butter
2 tablespoons almond butter
2 tablespoons chopped fresh flat-leaf parsley
¼ cup toasted sliced almonds

Blistered Beans with Ginger, Black Garlic and Cashews

This dish of quick stir-fried summer beans, blistered in super-sizzling hot oil and served with fermented black garlic, with its unique flavour, is out of this world. Fermented garlic brings a sweet, earthy, umami-packed punch to vegetables. It has notes of aged balsamic and caramel that work wonderfully with the beans, hoisin, orange and toasted cashews.

Black garlic is available in a number of forms, from whole heads to peeled cloves to a dehydrated powder. Look for it in specialty spice shops, Asian markets and health food stores.

1. Heat 2 tablespoons of the canola oil in a large nonstick skillet over high heat. When the oil is hot, add the green beans and toss to coat well with the oil. Cook and stir until the beans are bright in colour and have started to blister. Transfer the beans to a medium bowl.
2. Reduce the heat to medium and to the same pan, add the remaining 1 tablespoon canola oil, the onion, ginger, black garlic and chili. Cook, stirring frequently, until the onions start to soften, about 2 minutes. Return the green beans to the pan and toss together.
3. In a small bowl, stir together the hoisin sauce, soy sauce and orange zest. Pour the sauce over the beans and cook, stirring, until the sauce glazes the beans, 1 to 2 minutes. Add the toasted cashews, toss together, and season with salt and pepper. Transfer to a shallow serving bowl.

SERVES 4 TO 6

3 tablespoons canola oil, divided
1 pound (450 g) green beans, trimmed
½ small white onion, thinly sliced
1 (2-inch piece) peeled fresh ginger, thinly sliced lengthwise
6 to 8 fermented black garlic cloves, mashed with a fork
½ red Fresno chili, thinly sliced
3 tablespoons Hoisin Sauce (page 239 or store-bought)
2 tablespoons soy sauce
Zest of 1 orange
½ cup toasted cashews, roughly chopped
Kosher salt and freshly ground black pepper

Brussels Sprouts, Bacon and Toasted Fregola

Brussels sprouts are a divisive vegetable—either you are a fan or you heartily object. If you are not a fan, that's likely because you've had them either wildly overcooked or wildly undercooked. Therein lies the beauty of this dish. The leaves of these plump miniature cabbages are cooked just long enough to bring out their innate sweetness. Tossed in a sizzling hot pan with bacon and toasty fregola, and then showered with fresh Parmesan cheese, here's a side no one can possibly object to.

Fregola, sometimes called Sardinian couscous, is a pasta with a nutty flavour and irregular texture that is all its own. Use it where you would couscous or orzo, adding a toasted dimension to hot and cold side dishes.

SERVES 4 TO 6

1 cup dried fregola pasta
4 slices thick-cut bacon, diced
2 tablespoons unsalted butter
1 tablespoon olive oil
2 shallots, thinly sliced
1 clove garlic, minced
2 cups Brussels sprout leaves
Kosher salt and freshly ground black pepper
½ cup Roasted Chicken Stock (page 237) or Vegetable Stock (page 238) or store-bought
¼ cup grated Parmesan cheese
2 tablespoons chopped fresh flat-leaf parsley

1. Bring a large pot of salted water to a boil. Add the pasta and cook, stirring occasionally, until al dente, 10 to 12 minutes. Drain and transfer to a baking sheet.

2. In a large skillet over medium-high heat, cook the bacon until just about crisp, 2 to 3 minutes. Add the butter, olive oil, shallots and garlic and cook for about 1 minute. Add the Brussels sprout leaves and pasta. Season with salt and pepper. Cook, stirring frequently, until the leaves begin to wilt, 2 to 3 minutes. Add the chicken stock and mix well. Continue to cook for 2 minutes, until the liquid has evaporated. Toss in the Parmesan and parsley. Serve in a shallow serving bowl.

Cannellini Bean, Kale and Tomato Ragout

This Tuscan recipe is typically served with grilled meats. It is a sensational one-pot wonder with deep flavour and is completely satisfying.

Kale is usually sold in bunches tied around the stalks. Look for young tender, firm and fresh-looking leaves with thin stalks.

SERVES 4 TO 6

1. In a large skillet, melt 2 tablespoons of the butter in the olive oil over medium heat. Add the garlic and onion and cook, stirring frequently, until the onion starts to soften, 3 to 4 minutes.
2. Add the chili flakes and tomatoes and bring to a boil, then add the beans. Simmer, uncovered, until sauce has thickened, 30 to 40 minutes.
3. Add the kale and simmer, stirring occasionally, for 5 minutes. Add the parsley and Parmesan and stir in the remaining 1 tablespoon butter. Season with salt and pepper.

3 tablespoons unsalted butter, divided
1 tablespoon olive oil
4 cloves garlic, minced
1 yellow onion, finely diced
¼ teaspoon red chili flakes
1 can (14 ounces/398 mL) diced tomatoes
1 can (19 ounces/540 mL) cannellini beans, drained and rinsed
1 bunch of Tuscan kale, tough stems removed, chopped
¼ cup fresh flat-leaf parsley leaves, chopped
¼ cup grated Parmesan cheese
Kosher salt and freshly ground black pepper

Cheese Soufflé

Nothing could be easier than making a soufflé. For far too long, soufflés have struggled under the reputation of being difficult to make. A cheese soufflé is a classic recipe from the French kitchen. It is golden on the outside and soft, fluffy and so cheesy on the inside, and you will be making it again and again. The soufflé is made possible by the magic of one of our favourite ingredients in our home—the perfect egg.

By adding cooked spinach or Dungeness crab, you will raise this soufflé to a hallmark dish of the French culinary tradition.

1. Preheat the oven to 400°F. Melt the butter in a medium saucepan. Use 2 tablespoons of the butter to brush an 8-inch soufflé dish or deep round baking dish.

2. Stir the flour into the remaining butter. Cook, whisking, over medium heat until golden brown, 1 to 2 minutes, then whisk in the warm milk. Cook, stirring constantly, until the mixture thickens, 3 to 4 minutes. Add the salt, pepper, mustard, Parmesan, Gruyère and cheddar and stir until the cheese is melted. Remove from the heat and allow to cool slightly.

3. In a stand mixer fitted with the whisk attachment (or with an electric hand mixer and a large bowl), beat the egg whites until stiff peaks form, 4 to 5 minutes.

4. Whisk the egg yolks into the cheese mixture, and then gently but thoroughly fold the egg whites into the cheese mixture a third at a time. Pour into the prepared baking dish and bake for 30 minutes, until golden brown and set. Serve immediately.

SERVES 4 TO 6

5 tablespoons unsalted butter
3 tablespoons all-purpose flour
1 cup whole milk, warm
1 teaspoon kosher salt
½ teaspoon freshly ground black pepper
½ teaspoon dry mustard
1 cup grated Parmesan cheese
½ cup grated Gruyère cheese
½ cup grated aged cheddar cheese
5 large eggs, separated

Corn, Zucchini and Cheddar Sauté

Sweet corn kernels and zucchini sautéed in a hot pan until charred, then mixed with My Old Bay Seasoning and aged cheddar cheese, is a dish that celebrates the simple, fresh flavours of summer. It is hands down the best way to prepare corn.

There is no need to pull back the husk when choosing corn. Instead, choose ears that have brown tassels that are a little sticky to the touch. If the tassels look black or feel dry, that ear is old. Choose corn that feels firm with plump, even kernels.

1. Heat the olive oil in a large skillet over medium-high heat. Add the corn, zucchini, shallots, chili, garlic and Old Bay seasoning (if using) and sauté until the corn is tender, about 10 minutes.
2. Stir in the cream and cook, stirring occasionally, until slightly thickened, about 3 minutes. Add the cheddar and parsley and stir until the cheese has melted. Season to taste with salt and pepper. Transfer to a serving bowl.

SERVES 4 TO 6

2 tablespoons olive oil
2 cups fresh corn kernels (from 4 cobs)
2 cups diced zucchini
2 tablespoons chopped shallots
½ red Fresno chili, thinly sliced
2 teaspoons minced garlic
1 teaspoon My Old Bay Seasoning (page 229 or store-bought; optional)
½ cup heavy (35%) cream
½ cup grated aged white cheddar cheese
2 tablespoons chopped fresh flat-leaf parsley
Kosher salt and freshly ground black pepper

Creamy Spinach Parmesan Orzo

This creamy, cheesy dish is an exceptionally satisfying side. So much so, we recommend making double what you think you will need. Cauliflower, Parmesan and shallots cooked in a rosemary cream sauce, then tossed with spinach and orzo (a rice-shaped pasta), all adds up to risotto-like yumminess.

1. Bring a large pot of salted water to a boil. Add the pasta and cook until al dente, 8 to 10 minutes. Drain, then spread out evenly on a baking sheet.
2. In the same pot, heat the butter over medium-high heat. Add the shallots and cook, stirring frequently, until softened, about 2 minutes. Add the cauliflower, cream and rosemary, and season with salt and pepper. Bring to a boil, reduce the heat and simmer, stirring occasionally, until the cauliflower is cooked and the cream has thickened slightly, about 15 minutes.
3. Add the spinach and cream cheese and stir until the spinach has just wilted and the cheese has melted, about 1 minute. Stir in the pasta and Parmesan and season with salt and pepper. Transfer to a serving bowl.

SERVES 4 TO 6

1 cup dried orzo pasta
2 tablespoons unsalted butter
2 shallots, finely diced
2 cups roughly chopped cauliflower
2 cups heavy (35%) cream
½ sprig fresh rosemary, leaves roughly chopped
Kosher salt and freshly ground black pepper
2 cups loosely packed baby spinach
¼ cup cream cheese, at room temperature
½ cup grated Parmesan cheese

Gai Lan with Chili Jam

"Eat your greens" takes on an exhilarating twist when you have gai lan (Chinese broccoli) at the ready. This vibrant, crunchy, intensely flavoured side dish is buoyed by Hoisin Sauce and Chili Jam.

You can swap in any Asian green or combination. Try Shanghai bok choy, Chinese napa cabbage, yau choy, mustard greens, water spinach, tatsoi, watercress or pea shoots.

1. Heat the canola oil in large skillet over medium-high heat. When the oil is hot, add the bell pepper and garlic and sauté until the garlic is golden, about 2 minutes.
2. Add the gai lan, hoisin sauce and chicken stock, and toss to coat. Cover and cook until the gai lan is crisp-tender, 3 to 4 minutes. Uncover, stir in the chili jam and cook until the liquid has thickened, 1 to 2 minutes. Transfer to a serving dish.

SERVES 4 TO 6

2 tablespoons canola oil
1 red bell pepper, julienned
2 cloves garlic, thinly sliced
2 bunches of gai lan (about 1 pound/450 g), ends trimmed
3 tablespoons Hoisin Sauce (page 239 or store-bought)
¼ cup Roasted Chicken Stock (page 237 or store-bought)
¼ to ½ cup Chili Jam (page 231)

Harissa-Roasted Parsnips with Whipped Feta, Pistachios and Rosemary Honey

Parsnips have a wonderful nutty and floral flavour. When tender sweet parsnips are paired with spicy, smoky harissa spice, they instantly liven up. Hot and caramelized from the oven, the parsnips settle beautifully on top of the creamy whipped feta, topped with a good drizzle of rosemary honey and lots of pistachios.

1. Preheat the oven to 425°F. Line a baking sheet with parchment paper.
2. Place the parsnips in a large bowl and add the olive oil, ginger, harissa paste, and salt and pepper to taste. Toss to coat well. Arrange the parsnips in a single layer on the prepared baking sheet, making sure they have a little room on the sides to brown and caramelize. Roast until the parsnips are starting to turn golden brown on the edges, 20 to 25 minutes. Toss the parsnips to redistribute, and then continue to roast until tender and golden, another 5 to 10 minutes.
3. In a small bowl, combine the feta, cream and lemon juice. Mash with a fork or using a handheld blend, blend until smooth. Season with salt and pepper.
4. Spoon the whipped feta mixture onto a serving plate, top with the roasted parsnips, drizzle with rosemary honey and sprinkle with the pistachios.

SERVES 4 TO 6

1½ to 2 pounds (675 to 900 g) parsnips, peeled and sliced in half lengthwise
3 tablespoons olive oil
1 teaspoon finely grated peeled fresh ginger
1 teaspoon Harissa Paste (page 233 or store-bought)
Kosher salt and freshly ground black pepper
3 ounces (85 g) feta cheese
¼ cup heavy (35%) cream
1 teaspoon lemon juice
Rosemary Honey (page 235)
¼ cup pistachios, finely chopped

Hoisin-Glazed Eggplant with Sesame Miso Baba Ganoush

A thick slather of hoisin sauce on the sautéed Japanese eggplant gives it a rich and savoury depth of flavour, which pairs perfectly with the smoky umami-packed eggplant-miso purée. This is the best eggplant dynamic duo we know.

MAKE THE SESAME MISO BABA GANOUSH

1. Prepare the grill for direct cooking over medium heat (or preheat the oven to 450°F and line a baking sheet with parchment paper).
2. If using the grill, grill the eggplant, turning frequently, until it softens and the skin is well charred, about 30 minutes. Let cool. (Alternatively, if using the oven, cut the eggplant in half lengthwise. Place the eggplant halves cut side down on the prepared baking sheet and roast until tender, about 30 minutes. Remove from the oven and let sit until cool enough to handle.)
3. When the eggplant is cool, scoop out the flesh and place in a food processor. Add the olive oil, miso, tahini, sesame oil, paprika, and lemon zest and juice. Process until smooth, adding a little water, if necessary, to achieve desired consistency. Season with salt and pepper.

MAKE THE HOISIN-GLAZED EGGPLANT

4. In a large skillet, heat 3 tablespoons of the canola oil over high heat. Add the eggplant and cook, stirring frequently, until tender and golden brown, about 5 minutes. Transfer the eggplant to a large bowl.
5. Return the pan to high heat and add the remaining 2 tablespoons canola oil. Add the garlic, green onions and ginger and cook, stirring, until fragrant, about 30 seconds. Return the eggplant to the pan and stir to combine.
6. In a small bowl, whisk together the hoisin sauce, soy sauce, sesame oil and rice vinegar. Add the hoisin mixture to the pan and stir to coat the eggplant. Stir in the spinach and remove from the heat.
7. Spoon the baba ganoush onto a serving platter. Top with the hoisin-glazed eggplant and garnish with the pecans.

SERVES 4 TO 5

Sesame Miso Baba Ganoush

1 medium globe or Italian eggplant (about 1 pound/450 g)
2 tablespoons olive oil
2 tablespoons white miso
2 tablespoons tahini
1 teaspoon toasted sesame oil
1 teaspoon smoked paprika
Zest and juice of ½ lemon
Kosher salt and freshly ground black pepper

Hoisin-Glazed Eggplant

5 tablespoons canola oil, divided
4 small Japanese eggplants, cut into 1-inch pieces
2 cloves garlic, minced
1 bunch of green onions, chopped
1 tablespoon minced peeled fresh ginger
¼ cup Hoisin Sauce (page 239 or store-bought)
3 tablespoons soy sauce
1 tablespoon sesame oil
1 tablespoon seasoned rice vinegar
1 cup loosely packed baby spinach

¼ cup toasted pecans, chopped, for garnish

Pea Shoot and Sweet Pea Sauté with Pancetta and Lemon

Sweet garden peas are tangled in a web of pea shoots with well-seasoned cured pancetta adding a salty richness. Butter and lemon purée combine to create an aromatic and luscious glaze.

Snap peas and snow peas do not like being left out, and both would certainly be a lovely crisp addition to this dish.

1. In a large skillet, combine the olive oil and pancetta over medium-high heat. Cook the pancetta, stirring occasionally, until just crispy, about 8 minutes.
2. Add the shallots and peas and cook, stirring frequently, until hot, about 2 minutes. Add the butter and the lemon purée, mixing well. When the butter has melted, add the pea shoots, toss together, and season with salt and pepper. When the pea shoots have just wilted, transfer the mixture to a serving bowl.

SERVES 4 TO 6

1 tablespoon olive oil
2 ounces (57 g) pancetta (or 2 slices thick-cut bacon), diced
2 shallots, finely diced
2 cups fresh or frozen peas
2 tablespoons unsalted butter
1 tablespoon Lemon Purée (page 235)
2 cups pea shoots or baby spinach
Kosher salt and freshly ground black pepper

Polenta with Butternut Squash, Swiss Chard and Mascarpone

Dreamy, creamy, luscious polenta is quite easy to achieve if you know that the secret ingredient is cheese. It keeps the cornmeal soft and light while infusing it with an intense cheese depth. Topped with tender butternut squash, Swiss chard and mascarpone, this heavenly concoction appears elaborate and fanciful but it is an absolute breeze to pull together.

You can find quality medium ground cornmeal or instant polenta at your local grocer, Italian grocers and bulk stores.

1. Preheat the oven to 400°F. Line a baking sheet with parchment paper.
2. In a large bowl, toss the butternut squash with the olive oil and season with salt and pepper. Spread the squash in an even layer on the prepared baking sheet and roast until tender, about 30 minutes. Set aside.
3. In a medium saucepan, combine the water and 2 cups of the milk and bring to a boil over medium-high heat. Slowly pour in the polenta in an even stream, whisking continuously, and cook, whisking, until the polenta begins to thicken, 1 to 2 minutes. Reduce the heat to low and cook, whisking constantly, until the polenta is thick and creamy, 4 to 5 minutes. Remove from the heat, add the cheddar cheese, cream cheese and Parmesan and whisk until combined. Season with salt and pepper. Cover to keep warm until ready to serve.
4. Heat a large skillet over medium-high heat. Add the butter, shallots, garlic, capers and anchovies, if using. Stir together for 1 minute, until the shallots and garlic have softened. Add the Swiss chard, rosemary and roasted squash and toss together. Season with salt and pepper.
5. In a small bowl, combine the mascarpone and the remaining 3 tablespoons milk and whisk until smooth. Season with salt and pepper.
6. Spoon the polenta onto a serving platter. Top with the squash mixture and mascarpone mixture.

SERVES 4 TO 6

2 cups butternut squash cut into 1-inch cubes
2 tablespoons olive oil
Kosher salt and freshly ground black pepper
2 cups water
2 cups + 3 tablespoons whole milk, divided
1 cup instant polenta
½ cup grated cheddar cheese
¼ cup cream cheese, at room temperature
¼ cup grated Parmesan cheese
2 tablespoons unsalted butter
2 tablespoons finely diced shallots
2 large cloves garlic, minced
2 tablespoons drained capers, chopped
2 anchovy fillets, finely chopped (optional)
3 cups roughly chopped Swiss chard, stemmed
1 teaspoon minced fresh rosemary
½ cup mascarpone cheese, at room temperature

Potato Aloo Chaat with Tamarind Chutney, Cilantro Yogurt and Bhel Puri

The Indian vegetarian dish aloo chaat is a very popular street food combining potatoes, spices and sweet-and-sour chutneys. This creative dish is both comforting and enticing. Crispy spiced potatoes love cilantro. Mint in the yogurt is bright and fresh, and our Tamarind Date Paste lends a sweet-sour flavour.

Sweet potatoes work equally well in this recipe.

MAKE THE CILANTRO YOGURT

1. In a blender, combine the yogurt, lime juice, honey, chili, cilantro and mint; blend until smooth. Season with salt and pepper. Scrape into a small bowl, cover and refrigerate for up to 2 days.

MAKE THE POTATO ALOO CHAAT

2. Preheat the oven to 400°F. Line a baking sheet with parchment paper.
3. In a large bowl, combine the potatoes, olive oil, thyme sprigs, garlic, cumin, chili powder, and salt and pepper to taste. Toss well to coat. Spread on the prepared baking sheet and roast, stirring occasionally to ensure even browning, until the potatoes are fork-tender and golden brown, about 25 minutes.
4. Transfer the roasted potatoes to a large bowl. Toss with the tamarind date paste. Season with salt and pepper.
5. Transfer to a serving platter and spoon some of the cilantro yogurt over the potatoes. Sprinkle with the bhel puri and cilantro. Serve the remaining cilantro yogurt in a small bowl on the side.

SERVES 4 TO 6

Cilantro Yogurt (makes 1½ cups)
¾ cup plain full-fat Greek yogurt, more if needed
1 teaspoon lime juice
1 teaspoon honey
½ to 1 small green chili, stem and seeds removed
2 cups packed fresh cilantro leaves and stems, chopped
1 cup fresh mint leaves
Kosher salt and freshly ground black pepper

Potato Aloo Chaat
1 to 1½ pounds (450 to 675 g) mini Yukon Gold potatoes, scrubbed and cut in half
3 tablespoons olive oil
4 sprigs fresh thyme
3 cloves garlic, smashed
¼ teaspoon ground cumin
¼ teaspoon chili powder
Kosher salt and freshly ground black pepper
⅓ cup Tamarind Date Paste (page 234)

Garnishes
¾ cup bhel puri (Indian dry snack mix)
Fresh cilantro leaves

Roasted Cauliflower with Ricotta Salata and Lemon Caper Rémoulade

Cauliflower has risen to star status in recent years. We have always been fans, especially of the heirloom varieties. Aside from traditional white, you can now buy orange, green and magenta varieties to transform your meals into a veritable vegetable bouquet. In this dish, the caramelized edges of the roasted cauliflower are punched up with a tart, briny lemon caper rémoulade, salty ricotta and nutty pine nuts. Suddenly this formerly bland brassica gets top billing!

Customize roasted cauliflower with your favourite seasonings. You can herb-roast the cauliflower with olive oil and a little Parmesan or roast it with Furikake Seasoning (page 232).

1. Preheat the oven to 400°F. Line a baking sheet with parchment paper.
2. In a large bowl, combine the cauliflower, olive oil, capers, thyme, chili, lemon zest and juice, and salt and pepper to taste. Toss to coat.
3. Spread the cauliflower a single layer on the prepared baking sheet. Roast until golden brown and crispy, about 30 minutes, stirring once halfway through the cooking time. Transfer to a serving platter, drizzle with the rosemary honey and garnish with the ricotta salata, pine nuts and lemon caper rémoulade.

SERVES 4 TO 6

1 large head cauliflower, cut into florets (about 6 cups)
¼ cup olive oil
2 tablespoons drained capers
2 sprigs fresh thyme, leaves only, roughly chopped
1 Fresno chili, thinly sliced
Zest and juice of 1 lemon
Kosher salt and freshly ground black pepper
2 tablespoons Rosemary Honey (page 235)
¼ cup thinly shaved ricotta salata or Parmesan cheese
¼ cup pine nuts, toasted
½ cup Lemon Caper Rémoulade (page 245)

Roasted Oyster Mushrooms with Miso Garlic Butter and Miso Brittle

Oyster mushrooms are so stunning in both taste and appearance that we had to give them their very own dish. This is one of the most frequently made sides at our house. We know what you're thinking: just mushrooms? Umami-loaded and slathered in chili miso garlic butter—they're so good!

Sorrel is a leafy herb with a lemony flavour that brightens anything it is added to.

MAKE THE MISO BRITTLE

1. Place a rack in the lowest position in the oven. Preheat the oven to 170°F. Line a baking sheet with parchment paper or a silicone mat.
2. In a small bowl, stir together the miso and gochujang into a smooth paste.
3. Evenly spread the paste in a very thin layer on the prepared baking sheet and bake until completely dry, 1 to 2 hours. Let cool on the baking sheet. When cool, break into small flakes. Use immediately or store in a jar at room temperature for up to 2 months.

MAKE THE ROASTED OYSTER MUSHROOMS WITH MISO GARLIC BUTTER

4. Preheat the oven to 425°F.
5. Heat the olive oil in a large ovenproof skillet over medium-high heat. Add the butter, miso, garlic and chili, stir together, and cook for 1 minute. Add the mushrooms and toss to coat with the miso garlic butter. Season with salt and pepper. Transfer the skillet to the oven and roast, basting occasionally, until the mushrooms are tender, deep golden and crispy in spots, 15 to 20 minutes.
6. Squeeze the lemon over the mushrooms and transfer to a serving platter. Sprinkle with the sorrel and lots of miso brittle.

SERVES 4 TO 6

Miso Brittle (makes about 1 cup flakes)
¼ cup white miso
¼ cup gochujang

Roasted Oyster Mushrooms with Miso Garlic Butter
2 tablespoons olive oil
4 tablespoons unsalted butter
1 tablespoon white miso
2 teaspoons minced garlic
½ Fresno chili, thinly sliced
1½ pounds (675 g) oyster mushrooms
Kosher salt and freshly ground black pepper
½ lemon
Fresh picked sorrel leaves or flat-leaf parsley leaves, roughly chopped, for garnish

Sake and Miso Braised Shallots

If you have not yet incorporated shallots into your cooking, this is the dish that you will remember as changing everything. Shallots have a hint of garlic to them, which already adds a nuanced heft to a dish, but braising them in sake and miso imparts a sweet umami depth that makes them particularly captivating.

1. Melt the butter in a large skillet over medium heat. Add the shallots, cut side down, and thyme. Season with salt and pepper and cook, stirring occasionally, until browned, 3 to 5 minutes. Add the sake and cook until the liquid is reduced by half, about 5 minutes. Stir in the cream, then partially cover with a lid and continue to cook until the shallots are very tender, about 10 minutes.

2. Meanwhile, in a small measuring cup or bowl, stir together the rice vinegar, miso and soy sauce.

3. Remove the lid from the skillet and continue to cook until the cream is reduced by two-thirds. When the sauce has thickened, stir in the miso mixture and the lemon zest and juice. Season with salt and pepper if needed. Discard the thyme sprigs. Spoon the shallots and sauce into a serving bowl. Garnish with the chives and parsley.

SERVES 4 TO 6

4 tablespoons unsalted butter
24 shallots, peeled and cut in half
   lengthwise
2 sprigs fresh thyme
Kosher salt and freshly ground black
   pepper
1 cup sake
¾ cup heavy (35%) cream
2 tablespoons rice wine vinegar
1 tablespoon miso
1 tablespoon soy sauce
Zest and juice of ½ lemon

Garnishes
Fresh chives, chopped
Fresh flat-leaf parsley, chopped

Savoy Cabbage with Shiitake Mushrooms, Sausage, Miso and Garlic

Savoy cabbage is the perfect cabbage for cooking because of its tender leaves, and it's often used in familiar recipes like cabbage rolls and coleslaw. We like to add spicy or sweet Italian sausage cooked down with mushrooms and miso to make an incredibly great-tasting side or stuffing.

This dish is also awesome tossed together with ramen noodles.

1. Heat the olive oil in a large skillet over medium-high heat. Add the garlic and shallots and cook, stirring frequently, until softened, 1 to 2 minutes. Add the ginger and sausage and cook, breaking up the sausage with a wooden spoon and stirring frequently, until the sausage is browned, crisp and cooked through, 6 to 8 minutes. Using a slotted spoon, transfer the sausage mixture to a large bowl. Keep the fat in the pan.

2. Increase the heat to high and add the mushrooms. Cook, tossing often, until browned and starting to release their juices, 3 to 4 minutes. Add the cabbage and cook, tossing often, until the cabbage is wilted and tender, 3 to 4 minutes. Stir in the soy sauce, rice vinegar and miso and cook for another 2 minutes.

3. Transfer the cabbage mixture to the bowl with the sausage. Stir in the chives and chili. Transfer to a serving platter.

SERVES 4 TO 6

2 tablespoons olive oil
1 clove garlic, minced
2 shallots, thinly sliced
1 (1-inch) piece fresh ginger, peeled and finely grated
8 ounces (225 g) hot or sweet Italian sausage, casings removed
1 pound (450 g) shiitake mushrooms, thinly sliced (about 2 cups)
½ head savoy cabbage, thinly sliced
2 tablespoons soy sauce
1 tablespoon unseasoned rice vinegar
1 teaspoon white miso
⅓ cup thinly sliced fresh chives
½ red chili pepper, thinly sliced

Spätzle with Bacon and Gruyère

If you have never made spätzle, get ready to make it rain! This tiny, tender egg noodle is made by grating the dough into boiling water. At home, we use a perforated hotel pan, but using a colander or sieve yields the same pro results.

What makes spätzle stand out from other pasta are its pillowy consistency (similar to gnocchi, but not as dense or chewy) and its ability to take on bold flavours. Lots of caramelized onions, bacon and Gruyère cheese transform the spätzle into a creamy dish so good that it might move up the ranks to a main.

1. In a large bowl, whisk together the milk and eggs. Add the flour, salt and pepper and mix together until smooth. Cover and refrigerate for 30 minutes.
2. Bring a large pot of salted water to a boil. Hold a colander with large holes over the water. Add about half of the batter to the colander, press it into the simmering water using a rubber spatula and cook the noodles until firm, 2 to 3 minutes. Immediately transfer the spätzle to a baking sheet and drizzle with the olive oil to coat lightly. Repeat to use the remaining batter, then drain.
3. In a large skillet over medium-high heat, cook the bacon until light golden brown, 3 to 4 minutes. Reduce the heat to low, add the onion and cook, stirring occasionally, until caramelized, 10 to 12 minutes. Add the spätzle, Gruyère and dill and toss together. Season with salt and pepper. Transfer to a large serving dish.

SERVES 4 TO 6

1 cup whole milk or water
4 large eggs
2¼ cups all-purpose flour
2 teaspoons kosher salt, more for seasoning
¼ teaspoon freshly ground black pepper, more for seasoning
1 tablespoon olive oil
2 slices thick-cut bacon, diced
1 yellow onion, thinly sliced
½ cup grated Gruyère cheese (about 2 ounces/57 g)
2 tablespoons chopped fresh dill

Sunchokes Bravas with Chorizo and Romesco Sauce

Move over, potatoes. Sunchokes are ready to take the spotlight. Also known as Jerusalem artichoke, earth apple and sunroot, this hearty tubular root vegetable, related to sunflowers, delivers a potatoey vibe but is nuttier and slightly crunchier.

This spin on the Spanish tapas *patatas bravas* employs crispy golden sunchokes infused with an intense smokiness and crumbled spicy sausage tossed in romesco sauce, all crowned with a creamy arugula aioli. These crispy, flavour-packed nuggets are a standout on their own, but serve some eggs alongside and you have yourself one show-stopping brunch dish.

MAKE THE ROMESCO SAUCE

1. Set the oven to broil.
2. In a large bowl, toss together the tomatoes, bell pepper, red onion, garlic and olive oil. Season with salt and pepper. Spread the vegetables evenly on a baking sheet and broil until tender and very lightly charred in spots, 3 to 4 minutes.
3. Transfer the vegetables to a food processor. Add the almonds, parsley, sherry vinegar, paprika and chili flakes, then purée until smooth. Transfer to a small saucepan and season with salt and pepper. Set aside.

ROAST THE SUNCHOKES AND CHORIZO SAUSAGE

4. Preheat the oven to 400°F. Line a baking sheet with parchment paper.
5. On the baking sheet, toss the sunchokes and chorizo with the olive oil, thyme, lemon zest, and salt and pepper to taste. Spread out evenly. Roast for 25 minutes, then turn and roast for another 10 to 15 minutes, until the sunchokes are golden and crispy.

MEANWHILE, MAKE THE ARUGULA AIOLI

6. While the sunchokes are roasting, in a food processor, combine the mayonnaise, arugula, lemon juice, mustard and garlic. Purée until smooth. Season with salt and pepper.
7. To serve, heat the romesco sauce over medium heat. Toss the hot sunchokes and chorizo with the sauce. Transfer to a serving platter. Scatter the arugula over the top and drizzle with the arugula aioli.

SERVES 4 TO 6

Romesco Sauce
6 to 8 plum tomatoes, each cut into 4 wedges
1 red bell pepper, cut into ½-inch slices
½ red onion, cut into ½-inch wedges
2 cloves garlic, peeled
2 tablespoons olive oil
Kosher salt and freshly ground black pepper
¼ cup raw almonds
¼ cup fresh flat-leaf parsley leaves
1 tablespoon sherry vinegar
1 teaspoon smoked paprika
½ teaspoon red chili flakes

Roasted Sunchokes and Chorizo
2 pounds (900 g) sunchokes, scrubbed and cut in half
2 dry-cured chorizo sausage (2 ounces/57 g each), cut into ¼-inch coins
¼ cup extra-virgin olive oil
2 sprigs fresh thyme, leaves only
Zest of 1 lemon
Kosher salt and freshly ground black pepper

Arugula Aioli
¾ cup mayonnaise
1 cup packed baby arugula
2 tablespoons lemon juice
1 tablespoon Dijon mustard
1 teaspoon minced garlic
Kosher salt and freshly ground black pepper

1 cup baby arugula, for serving

Tempura Broccolini with Curry Leaf Mayonnaise

Open our fridge and you will always find broccoli. However, we are also big fans of its counterpart broccolini, which is a cross between broccoli and gai lan (Chinese broccoli). With a wonderful mellow, almost sweet broccoli flavour and pleasant texture, we think it is just perfect to use. Topped with a tomato mint chutney and creamy aromatic curry mayonnaise, this exotic green immediately catapulted to the top of weekly requests.

Broccolini does not require a lot of prep, just a quick trim of the stems. It is great sautéed quickly with some olive oil, chili, soy sauce and ginger or charred on the grill and finished with garlic butter and lemon.

MAKE THE CURRY LEAF MAYONNAISE

1. In a small bowl, whisk together the ingredients until smooth. Use immediately or store in an airtight container in the refrigerator for up to 2 weeks.

MAKE THE TEMPURA BROCCOLINI

2. In a medium bowl, whisk together the flour, cornstarch, baking powder and salt. Whisk in the sparkling water until just combined.
3. Line a plate with paper towel. In a deep medium saucepan, heat 4 inches of vegetable oil to 375°F over medium-high heat. Working in batches, dip the broccolini stems one at a time into the batter, then carefully place in the hot oil and deep-fry until crisp and golden, about 3 minutes, turning halfway through cooking until both sides are golden brown. Using a slotted spoon, transfer the broccolini to the paper towel to drain and season lightly with salt and pepper.
4. Arrange the broccolini tempura on a serving platter and serve the curry leaf mayonnaise and tomato mint chutney on the side.

SERVES 4 TO 6

Curry Leaf Mayonnaise (makes 1 cup)
1 cup mayonnaise
1 tablespoon lemon juice
1 tablespoon black mustard seeds
1 teaspoon crushed dried curry leaves
¼ teaspoon ground turmeric
⅛ teaspoon Kashmiri chili powder
⅛ teaspoon kosher salt

Tempura Broccolini
1 cup all-purpose flour
¼ cup cornstarch
1 teaspoon baking powder
½ teaspoon kosher salt, more for seasoning
1¼ cups sparkling water
Vegetable oil, for deep-frying
2 bunches of broccolini, trimmed
Kosher salt and freshly ground black pepper

Tomato Mint Chutney (page 76), for serving

Leek and Spinach Pie

Spinach and leeks are definitely in the right place snuggled under a blanket of airy, crispy, flaky phyllo. This is our version of spanakopita, minus the fussy folding. We cannot seem to get enough of this savoury, salty, ridiculously delectable pie.

1. Preheat the oven to 350°F.

MAKE THE FILLING

2. In a large skillet over medium heat, melt the butter with the olive oil. Add the leeks and cook, stirring frequently, until softened, 3 to 4 minutes. Add the garlic and za'atar and continue cooking, stirring frequently, for 2 minutes. Increase the heat to medium-high, add the cream and cook until it is reduced by half, 3 to 4 minutes. Stir in the spinach in batches until wilted. Remove from the heat.

3. Add the crumbled feta, ricotta and dill and mix well. Season with salt and pepper. Pour the filling into a 13 x 9-inch baking dish.

PREPARE THE PASTRY AND ASSEMBLE

4. Lay 1 sheet of phyllo on a cutting board. Brush with some of the melted butter. Lay another sheet of phyllo on top, brush with melted butter, and repeat to use the remaining phyllo and butter, brushing the top layer with butter. Trim the phyllo to fit the baking dish. Lay the phyllo sheets on top of the leek and spinach filling.

5. Using a sharp knife, score the dough in a diamond pattern. Sprinkle with the sesame seeds. Bake until golden brown and crispy, 15 to 20 minutes.

SERVES 4 TO 6

Filling

2 tablespoons unsalted butter
1 tablespoon olive oil
2 large leeks (white and light green parts only; outer layer discarded), diced
2 cloves garlic, minced
2 teaspoons Za'atar Spice (page 230 or store-bought)
1 cup heavy (35%) cream
2 pounds (900 g) baby spinach
3 ounces (85 g) feta cheese, crumbled (about 1 cup)
½ cup ricotta cheese
1 cup fresh dill, roughly chopped
Kosher salt and freshly ground black pepper

Pastry

6 sheets phyllo pastry
2 tablespoons unsalted butter, melted
1 teaspoon sesame seeds

Zucchini Parmesan Fritters with Hot Chili Honey

This is the perfect side dish or appetizer to make when you have an abundance of zucchini in your garden or kitchen. These addictive crispy cheesy fritters with their golden-brown crunch will be a smash hit.

Our Hot Chili Honey is also great for drizzling on everything from biscuits to chicken.

MAKE THE HOT CHILI HONEY

1. In a small saucepan, combine the butter, garlic and ginger. Cook over medium heat until fragrant, about 1 minute. Add the soy sauce, rice vinegar, sambal oelek and honey. Bring to a boil, stirring, and cook for 1 minute. Remove from the heat and allow to cool. Stir in the lemon zest and juice and green onion. Use immediately or store in an airtight container in the refrigerator for up to 1 week.

MAKE THE ZUCCHINI PARMESAN FRITTERS

2. In a large bowl, whisk together the flour and sparkling water until a smooth batter forms. Whisk in the eggs, one at a time, until incorporated. Stir in the Parmesan, mint and parsley. Gently fold in the zucchini.
3. Line a plate with paper towel. In a large skillet over medium-high heat, heat the vegetable oil to 325°F. Working in batches, add spoonfuls of the mixture to the hot oil. Do not crowd the pan. Fry until the bottom is golden brown, 2 to 3 minutes. Turn and fry until golden brown on the other side, about 2 minutes. Transfer the fritters to the paper towel to drain.
4. Arrange the zucchini fritters on a serving platter and season with sea salt. Garnish with the lemon wedges and serve the hot chili honey on the side.

SERVES 4 TO 6

Hot Chili Honey
1 tablespoon unsalted butter
2 teaspoons minced garlic
1 teaspoon minced peeled fresh ginger
2 teaspoons soy sauce
2 teaspoons rice wine vinegar
2 teaspoons sambal oelek
¼ cup honey
Zest and juice of ½ lemon
1 green onion, finely chopped

Zucchini Parmesan Fritters
¼ cup all-purpose flour
¼ cup sparkling water
3 large eggs
¼ cup grated Parmesan cheese
2 tablespoons chopped fresh mint
2 tablespoons chopped fresh flat-leaf parsley
4 zucchini, cut into matchsticks (about 4 cups)
1 cup vegetable oil, for deep-frying

For serving
Sea salt
Lemon wedges

DESSERTS

June's Famous Carrot Cake with Cream Cheese Frosting

Named after Lora's mom, June, this cake got its start when Lora was in cooking school and spent hours turning carrots, a classic French technique of peeling and shaping vegetables into a symmetrical barrel shape. Ever studious, she practised at home so much that she needed to find a way to use all the peelings. Thus was born this irresistible cake covered with a rich cream cheese frosting, which her family ate for months.

We know everyone has a go-to carrot cake recipe in their repertoire, but seriously June's is hands down the very best we have ever tasted. There is something just absolutely perfect about a recipe that comes from mom.

MAKE THE CANDIED CARROT CURLS (IF USING)

1. Preheat the oven to 200°F. Line a baking sheet with parchment paper or a silicone mat.
2. In a medium saucepan, bring the water and granulated sugar to a boil over high heat, then reduce the heat to a simmer. Add the carrots and simmer until tender, about 10 minutes.
3. Drain the carrots, pat dry and spread on the prepared baking sheet. Bake until crisp, 1½ to 2 hours. Use immediately or store in an airtight container at room temperature for up to 1 week.

MAKE THE CARROT CAKE

4. Preheat the oven to 375°F. Butter two 9-inch round cake pans and dust with flour, tapping out any excess.
5. Spread the walnuts in a single layer on a baking sheet and toast in the oven until lightly golden, about 7 minutes. Allow to cool. Finely chop the walnuts.
6. In a large bowl, sift together the flour, baking powder, baking soda, cinnamon and salt.
7. In a separate large bowl, whisk together the eggs and granulated sugar until thick. Add the vegetable oil and whisk until incorporated. Add the flour mixture and stir well. Fold in the grated carrots and walnuts until the mixture is smooth.
8. Divide the batter evenly between the prepared pans and bake for 1 hour, or until a cake tester inserted in the middle of the cakes comes out clean. Turn the cakes out onto a rack and cool completely before frosting.

MAKE THE CREAM CHEESE FROSTING

9. In a stand mixer fitted with the paddle attachment, beat the cream cheese on medium speed until smooth. Add the butter and beat until blended. Add the icing sugar, vanilla and lemon juice and beat until fluffy, about 3 minutes.

ASSEMBLE THE CAKE

10. Using a long serrated knife, cut the cooled cakes in half horizontally to create 4 layers. Place 1 cake layer cut side up on a cake plate. Using an offset spatula, spread a fifth of the frosting over the cake layer, spreading it right to the edge.
11. Carefully set the second cake layer cut side down on top and spread another fifth of the frosting over it. Repeat with remaining cake layers. Garnish with the candied carrot curls, if using. Use the remaining frosting to frost the sides. The cake can be stored, covered, in the refrigerator for up to 3 days.

SERVES 12

Candied Carrot Curls (optional)
1 cup water
1 cup extra-fine granulated sugar
1 cup very thinly sliced peeled carrots

Carrot Cake
1½ cups raw walnut halves
2 cups all-purpose flour
2 teaspoons baking powder
2 teaspoons baking soda
2 teaspoons cinnamon
1 teaspoon kosher salt
4 large eggs
2 cups granulated sugar
1½ cups vegetable oil
3½ cups grated peeled carrots

Cream Cheese Frosting
2 packages (8 ounces/225 g each) cream cheese, at room temperature
½ cup unsalted butter, at room temperature
2 cups icing sugar, sifted
1 tablespoon vanilla extract
1 tablespoon lemon juice

Chocolate Cherry Pavlova

This chocolaty meringue cake has a light and delicate crisp crust with a soft marshmallowy centre. A nod to Black Forest cake, with an enchanted trifecta of chocolate, bourbon-soaked cherries and whipped cream, this dessert is sure to be requested often.

The pavlova can be made a day or two in advance of serving and stored in a cool, dry place in an airtight container.

MAKE THE CHERRY SAUCE

1. In a medium saucepan, combine the cherries, orange juice, brown sugar and cinnamon. Bring to a boil over medium-high heat.

2. In a small bowl, stir together the cornstarch and bourbon. Stir into the cherries and cook, stirring constantly, until the sauce has thickened, about 1 minute. Remove from the heat and cool completely. Use immediately or store in an airtight container in the refrigerator for up to 2 weeks.

MAKE THE PAVLOVA

3. Preheat the oven to 350°F. Lightly spray a 9-inch springform pan with nonstick baking spray. Line the bottom and sides of the pan with parchment paper.

4. In a stand mixer fitted with the whisk attachment, beat the egg whites, lemon juice, vanilla and salt on medium speed until foamy. Increase the speed to medium-high and, while the mixer is running, slowly add the granulated sugar. Continue beating until stiff and glossy peaks form. Using a rubber spatula, carefully fold in the melted chocolate, trying to keep the egg whites as fluffy as possible.

5. Spoon the meringue into the prepared pan and smooth the top with an offset spatula. Bake for 40 minutes. Turn off the oven, keep the door closed, and leave the pavlova in the oven to finish cooking for another 30 minutes. The marshmallow centre will sink and leave high, crisp sides.

FINISH THE PAVLOVA

6. Just before serving, carefully remove the meringue from the springform pan and place on a serving plate. (The meringue can be stored covered at room temperature for 1 day, but best filled and served the day made.)

7. Beat the cream and icing sugar until soft peaks form. Place some of the whipped cream in the centre of the meringue, then spoon some of the cherry sauce over the top. Garnish with the chocolate shavings. Serve with the remaining cherry sauce and whipped cream on the side.

SERVES 8 TO 10

Cherry Sauce (makes 3 cups)
2 cups fresh or frozen pitted sweet cherries
½ cup orange juice
½ cup packed brown sugar
¼ teaspoon cinnamon
1 tablespoon cornstarch
2 tablespoons bourbon or water

Pavlova
4 egg whites
½ teaspoon lemon juice
½ teaspoon vanilla extract
Pinch of kosher salt
¾ cup granulated sugar
1 pound (450 g) dark chocolate, melted
1½ cups heavy (35%) cream, cold
3 tablespoons icing sugar
¼ cup dark chocolate shavings for garnish

Coconut Cream Pie with Candied Macadamia Nuts

The diner classic has stood the test of time thanks to its prize-winning peaks of cloud-like coconut-flecked cream, rich coconut custard and coconut graham crust. This creamy, dreamy coconut cream pie is a favourite dessert for entertaining. This coconut lover's dream on a plate likely will not last long, so dig in! We have perfected a classic and think it's incredible. We hope you love our version.

MAKE THE CANDIED MACADAMIA NUTS

1. Line a baking sheet with parchment paper. In a large sauté pan or skillet, combine the brown sugar, honey, butter and salt. Cook over medium-high heat, stirring constantly, until the mixture is melted and starting to bubble, 1 to 2 minutes. Stir in the macadamia nuts and cook, stirring, until the nuts are caramelized, 6 to 7 minutes. Scrape the candied nuts onto the prepared baking sheet and let cool completely, then roughly chop.

MAKE THE CRUST

2. Preheat the oven to 350°F.
3. In a large bowl, combine the graham cracker crumbs, shredded coconut, brown sugar, salt and melted butter. Stir until the mixture has the texture of wet sand. Transfer the mixture to a 9-inch pie plate and press it firmly and evenly across the bottom and up the sides of the pie plate. Place on a baking sheet and bake until the crust is set and the edges are brown, 10 to 12 minutes. Allow to cool.

MAKE THE FILLING

4. In a medium saucepan, combine the whole milk, coconut milk and shredded coconut. Heat over medium-high heat until the milk just begins to simmer. Remove from the heat, cover and let stand for 10 minutes. Strain, discarding the coconut, and return the milk to the saucepan.
5. In a medium bowl, whisk together the egg yolks, coconut sugar, cornstarch and vanilla until smooth. Gradually whisk the warm milk into the egg mixture to temper the eggs. Return the mixture to the saucepan. Heat the custard base over medium heat, whisking vigorously, until it starts to thicken, 1 to 2 minutes. Pour the custard into another medium bowl and immediately cover the surface with plastic wrap, making sure it is touching the whole surface of the custard to prevent a skin from forming on top. Let the custard cool to room temperature, then refrigerate until completely chilled, at least 1 hour.

MAKE THE WHIPPED CREAM

6. In a large bowl, whisk the cream with the icing sugar until medium to stiff peaks form.

TO FINISH

7. Spoon the chilled coconut custard into the pie crust. Top with the whipped cream and garnish with toasted coconut flakes and the candied macadamia nuts. The pie can be stored, covered, in the refrigerator for up to 2 days.

SERVES 8 TO 10

Candied Macadamia Nuts
¼ cup packed brown sugar
2 tablespoons honey
2 tablespoons unsalted butter
½ teaspoon kosher salt
1½ cups chopped macadamia nuts

Crust
2 cups graham cracker crumbs
1 cup sweetened shredded coconut
3 tablespoons brown sugar
Pinch of kosher salt
¼ cup unsalted butter, melted

Filling
2½ cups whole milk
1 can (14 ounces/400 mL) full-fat coconut milk
1 cup sweetened shredded coconut
6 egg yolks
½ cup coconut sugar
¼ cup cornstarch
1 teaspoon vanilla extract

Whipped Cream
1 cup heavy (35%) cream
3 tablespoons icing sugar

1 cup sweetened coconut flakes, toasted, for garnish

Old-Fashioned Doughnuts with Vanilla Glaze

We don't know about your family, but in our family we are obsessed with doughnuts. In every town or city we visit, we are on the hunt to find the most exceptionally glazed, filled, round, square and traditional doughnut we ever tasted. When we're at home, we make perfect little classic old-fashioned doughnuts dipped in a vanilla glaze.

These doughnuts are just as delicious rolled in cinnamon sugar. Combine ½ cup sugar and ½ teaspoon cinnamon in a large bowl. Dip the warm doughnuts in the sugar mixture to coat. Let sit for a few minutes, then coat a second time.

MAKE THE DOUGHNUTS

1. In a large bowl, sift together the cake flour, baking powder and salt.
2. In a stand mixer fitted with the paddle attachment, beat the butter and granulated sugar until sandy. Add the egg yolks and vanilla and mix until light and thick. Add the flour mixture to the butter mixture in 3 additions, alternating with 2 additions of the sour cream. Cover with plastic wrap and chill in the refrigerator for at least 1 hour before rolling out the dough.
3. On a lightly floured surface, roll out the dough to about ½-inch thickness. Using a doughnut cutter, cut out doughnuts, dipping the cutter in flour as necessary to prevent sticking. You should get about 12 doughnuts (and holes).
4. Line a plate with paper towel. In a large, heavy pot, heat 2 inches of canola oil to 325°F. When the oil is hot, deep-fry the doughnuts and holes, a few at a time, for about 2 minutes on each side, turning once halfway through, until golden brown. Using a slotted spoon, transfer the doughnuts and holes to the paper towel to drain. Allow to cool for 5 to 8 minutes before dipping in the glaze.

MAKE THE VANILLA GLAZE

5. While the doughnuts and holes are cooling, in a small bowl, stir together the ingredients until smooth.

GLAZE THE DOUGHNUTS AND HOLES

6. Dip the top of each doughnut and the holes into the glaze and place on a rack set on a baking sheet to catch excess glaze. The doughnuts can be stored, covered, at room temperature for up to 3 days.

MAKES ABOUT 12 DOUGHNUTS

Old-Fashioned Doughnuts
2¼ cups cake flour
2 tablespoons baking powder
1 teaspoon kosher salt
2 tablespoons unsalted butter, at room temperature
½ cup granulated sugar
3 egg yolks
1 teaspoon vanilla extract
½ cup sour cream
Canola oil, for deep-frying

Vanilla Glaze
1¼ cups icing sugar
1 tablespoon corn syrup
1 tablespoon unsalted butter, melted
1 tablespoon whole milk
½ teaspoon vanilla extract

Lora's Chocolate Cake with Chocolate Peanut Butter Frosting

Every family needs a winning chocolate cake in their collection, so we could not wait to share our absolute favourite with you. Chocolate and peanut butter are meant to be together. This is one of our more decadent cakes, smothered in a feathery, creamy peanut butter frosting, then covered in a velvety chocolate ganache.

MAKE THE CHOCOLATE GANACHE

1. In a heavy medium saucepan, heat the cream over low heat until warm. Add the chocolate chips and stir just until melted and the mixture is smooth. Do not let the mixture come to a boil. Transfer the mixture to a medium bowl, cover with plastic wrap and refrigerate until the ganache reaches a spreading consistency, about 1½ hours.

MAKE THE CHOCOLATE CAKE

2. Preheat the oven to 350°F. Lightly grease two 9-inch round cake pans.
3. In a large bowl, whisk together the flour, granulated sugar, cocoa powder, baking powder, baking soda, salt and instant coffee.
4. In a medium bowl, whisk together the milk, vegetable oil, eggs and vanilla. Add the milk mixture to the flour mixture and mix until well combined.
5. Whisk the boiling water into the batter until combined. Divide the batter evenly between the prepared pans, smooth the tops, and bake until a cake tester inserted in the middle of the cakes comes out clean, about 15 minutes. Remove from the oven and cool for 10 minutes in the pans. Turn the cakes out onto a rack and let cool completely.

MAKE THE CHOCOLATE PEANUT BUTTER FROSTING

6. In a stand mixer fitted with the paddle attachment, combine the cream cheese, peanut butter and butter. Beat on medium speed until smooth and creamy, scraping the bowl once or twice, 2 to 3 minutes.
7. In a large bowl, whisk together the icing sugar and cocoa powder until evenly combined and no lumps remain.
8. With the mixer on low speed, slowly add the icing sugar mixture to the cream cheese mixture, mixing until well blended. Increase the speed to high and beat until fluffy and creamy, about 15 seconds.

TO FINISH

9. Place 1 cake layer bottom side down on a serving plate. Spread the chocolate peanut butter frosting evenly over the cake. Place the second cake layer bottom side up on top. Spread the chocolate ganache over the cake, allowing it to run over the sides. Garnish with the shaved dark chocolate. The cake can be stored, covered, in the refrigerator for up to 3 days.

SERVES 12

Chocolate Ganache
1 cup heavy (35%) cream
1½ cups semisweet chocolate chips

Chocolate Cake
2 cups all-purpose flour
2 cups granulated sugar
¾ cup unsweetened cocoa powder
2 teaspoons baking powder
1½ teaspoons baking soda
1 teaspoon kosher salt
1 teaspoon instant coffee granules
1 cup whole milk
½ cup vegetable oil
2 large eggs
2 teaspoons vanilla extract
1 cup boiling water

Chocolate Peanut Butter Frosting
1 package (8 ounces/225 g) cream cheese, at room temperature
½ cup smooth peanut butter
4 tablespoons unsalted butter, at room temperature
3 cups icing sugar
½ cup unsweetened cocoa powder

Shaved dark chocolate, for garnish

Nutty Tart

Try this spin on a classic pecan pie. Our version has a buttery, toffee-like, gooey filling with a variety of toasted nuts in a sweet dough crust that is just perfect.

Our nutty tart is wonderful with a big scoop of our Vanilla Ice Cream (page 219) or on its own with a cup of tea. Sometimes we vary the recipe by adding ½ cup chocolate chips—very acceptable, in our opinion!

MAKE THE CRUST

1. Preheat the oven to 350°F. Butter a 14 x 4½-inch rectangular tart pan with removable bottom (or a 9-inch round tart pan with removable bottom).

2. In a stand mixer fitted with the paddle attachment, combine the butter, granulated sugar and egg. Beat just until blended. Add the flour and salt and beat until moist clumps form. Gather the dough into a ball. On a lightly floured surface, roll out the dough into a rectangle (or circle) large enough to fit the tart pan with a very slight overhang. Gently lift the dough into the tart pan and press the pastry onto the bottom and up the sides (but not into the creases) of the pan. With a sharp knife cut excess pastry from the top of the tart pan. Press the pastry into the creases of the pan.

3. Place the tart pan on a baking sheet. Line the tart shell with foil or parchment paper, leaving a 1-inch overhang, and fill with pie weights or dried beans. Bake until the edges are just beginning to turn golden all over, 15 to 20 minutes. Transfer to a rack and let cool completely, then remove parchment paper and pie weights.

MAKE THE FILLING

4. Melt the butter in a small saucepan over medium-high heat. Remove from the heat.

5. In a medium bowl, stir together the brown sugar, corn syrup, salt and vanilla. Whisk in the eggs, then whisk in the melted butter. Fold in the nuts. Place the tart pan on a baking sheet and pour the filling into the tart shell.

BAKE THE TART

6. Bake the tart, rotating the pan halfway through, until the filling is set around the edges and jiggles slightly in the centre when nudged, about 1 hour. Loosely place a tent of foil over the tart if the crust gets too dark. Transfer to a rack to cool completely. Remove the sides and dust with icing sugar just before serving. The tart can be stored, covered, in the refrigerator for up to 3 days.

SERVES 8

Crust

½ cup unsalted butter, cut into ½-inch cubes, at room temperature
⅔ cup granulated sugar
1 large egg
2 cups all-purpose flour
¼ teaspoon kosher salt

Filling

2 tablespoons unsalted butter
1 cup packed brown sugar
½ cup light corn syrup
1 teaspoon kosher salt
1 teaspoon vanilla extract
3 large eggs
1 cup assorted chopped roasted nuts (such as pistachios, hazelnuts, walnuts, pine nuts)

Icing sugar, for dusting

Pineapple Rum Cake

This timeless classic has changed a little over the years. While our grand-mothers would have relied on canned pineapple rings and maraschino cher-ries to decorate the cake, we use fresh pineapple and a little rum, and then bake the cake until it gets all sticky and caramelized.

This cake is wonderful served warm with Salted Caramel Sauce (page 212) poured over the top.

1. Preheat the oven to 350°F. Lightly grease a 9-inch round or square cake pan at least 2 inches deep.

PREPARE THE RUM PINEAPPLE

2. Melt the butter in a saucepan over medium-high heat. Add the pineapple and cook, stirring occasionally, until the juices have evaporated and the pineapple is nicely browned, 8 to 10 minutes. Stir in the honey and rum and cook, stirring frequently, until the pineapple is coated and sticky, 1 to 2 minutes. Remove from the heat and allow to cool while making the cake batter.

MAKE THE CAKE

3. In a large bowl, whisk together the eggs, sugar, melted butter and vanilla.
4. In a small bowl, whisk together the flour, baking powder and salt. Stir the flour mixture into the egg mixture alternately with the milk, beginning and ending with the flour, stirring thoroughly after each addition.
5. Pour the batter into the prepared pan. Evenly spoon the caramelized pineapple chunks and any accumulated juices over the top.
6. Bake the cake until light golden brown, 50 to 60 minutes. Remove from the oven and let cool in the pan for 10 to 15 minutes before serving. The cake can be stored, covered, at room temperature for 2 to 3 days.

SERVES 8

Rum Pineapple
2 tablespoons unsalted butter
½ fresh pineapple, peeled and cut into 2-inch chunks
2 tablespoons honey
1 tablespoon dark rum

Cake
2 large eggs
¾ cup granulated sugar
3 tablespoons unsalted butter, melted
1 teaspoon vanilla extract
1½ cups all-purpose flour
1½ teaspoons baking powder
½ teaspoon kosher salt
1 cup whole milk

Chocolate Fudge Brownies
with Salted Caramel Sauce

These brownies are rich, super moist, fudgy, unbelievably addictive and oh so chocolaty. Definitely a dessert that is worthy of being made every day.

Minus the Salted Caramel Sauce, these brownies pack extremely well into lunchboxes and are a terrific late-night snack.

MAKE THE CHOCOLATE FUDGE BROWNIES

1. Preheat the oven to 350°F. Line an 8-inch square cake pan with parchment paper.
2. Chop the chocolate into chunks. Melt half of the chocolate in the microwave in 20-second intervals, stirring after each interval. Set aside the remaining chocolate chunks.
3. In a large bowl, beat together the melted butter and sugar with an electric hand mixer until smooth. Beat in the eggs and vanilla until the mixture is fluffy and light in colour, 1 to 2 minutes.
4. Whisk in the melted chocolate (make sure it is not too hot or it will cook the eggs), then sift the flour, cocoa powder and salt over the mixture. Fold to incorporate the dry ingredients, being careful not to overmix, as this will cause the brownies to be more cake-like in texture.
5. Fold in the reserved chocolate chunks. Scrape the batter into the prepared baking pan and smooth the top. Bake for 20 to 25 minutes, until fudgy and set. Remove from the oven and cool completely in the pan. The brownies can be stored, covered, at room temperature for up to 3 days.

MAKE THE SALTED CARAMEL SAUCE

6. While the brownies are cooling, in a small saucepan, heat the sugar and water over medium heat to melt the sugar. Continue cooking and swirling (not stirring) the sugar until it turns amber. Whisk in the sea salt and cream. The mixture will briefly bubble up violently. Continue whisking until the sauce is smooth, about 2 minutes. Stir in the butter and vanilla. When the sauce is creamy and smooth, remove from the heat. Allow to cool. If not using right away, the sauce can be stored in a sealed container for up to 1 week.

TO FINISH

7. Serve the brownies topped with a scoop of vanilla ice cream and a drizzle of warm salted caramel sauce.

MAKES 9 BROWNIES

Chocolate Fudge Brownies
8 ounces (225 g) good-quality semisweet chocolate
¾ cup (1½ sticks) unsalted butter, melted
1¼ cups granulated sugar
2 large eggs
2 teaspoons vanilla extract
¾ cup all-purpose flour
¼ cup cocoa powder
1 teaspoon kosher salt

Salted Caramel Sauce (makes about 1 cup)
1 cup granulated sugar
¼ cup water
1 teaspoon sea salt
¾ cup heavy (35%) cream
3 tablespoons unsalted butter
1 teaspoon vanilla extract

Vanilla Ice Cream (page 219), for serving

Lemon Ricotta Cheesecake with Caramelized Figs and Pistachios

This whipped lemon ricotta cheesecake is rich and delicious. Whipped ricotta cheese with lemon and honey is baked in a flaky phyllo crust that creates wisps of crispness against the soft, creamy cheesecake. Honey, figs and pistachios is a match made in heaven and is the perfect decadent topping.

This wonderful year-round dessert can be accented with a variety of different ripe and seasonal fruits. Caramelized pears, peaches or cherries are all equally delicious.

MAKE THE LEMON RICOTTA CHEESECAKE

1. Preheat the oven to 350°F. Butter a 9-inch springform pan.
2. Place 1 sheet of the phyllo pastry on a work surface and brush with some melted butter. Lay another sheet of phyllo on top and brush with melted butter. Transfer the buttered phyllo sheets to the prepared pan and gently press them to fit inside the pan. Repeat 3 more times, overlapping each double layer, until you have completely covered the bottom and sides of the pan, with the phyllo sheets hanging over the edges. Brush the top sheet of phyllo with melted butter.
3. In a food processor, combine the ricotta and cream and process until smooth and creamy, 3 to 5 minutes. Add the honey, granulated sugar, eggs, egg yolks, vanilla and lemon juice and process until well combined, 2 to 3 minutes. Stir in the lemon zest. Pour the mixture into the phyllo-lined pan. Fold over the excess phyllo to completely cover the top of the cheesecake.
4. Bake for 1 hour. Turn off the oven and leave the cheesecake in the oven for 30 minutes. The cheesecake should be well set with some small cracks on the surface. Transfer to a rack and allow to cool completely.

MEANWHILE, MAKE THE CARAMELIZED FIGS

5. While the cheesecake is baking, melt the butter in a large nonstick skillet over medium heat. Sprinkle 1 tablespoon of the brown sugar over the melted butter. Place the figs in the pan cut side down and sprinkle with the remaining 1 tablespoon brown sugar. Cook until golden brown on the bottom, 2 to 3 minutes. Turn the figs over, remove from the heat and allow the figs to cool down in the pan.

TO FINISH

6. Garnish the cheesecake with the caramelized figs and pistachios. Drizzle with honey. The cheesecake can be stored, covered, in the refrigerator for up to 2 days.

SERVES 10 TO 12

Lemon Ricotta Cheesecake
8 sheets phyllo pastry
4 tablespoons unsalted butter, melted
2 pounds (900 g) ricotta cheese
¼ cup heavy (35%) cream
½ cup honey
½ cup granulated sugar
4 large eggs
2 egg yolks
2 teaspoons vanilla extract
Zest and juice of 1 lemon

Caramelized Figs
2 tablespoons unsalted butter
2 tablespoons brown sugar, divided
6 fresh figs, cut in half lengthwise

To finish
⅓ cup pistachios
Honey, for drizzling

Strawberry Ginger Trifle

We are bringing back the trifle! We don't know why these show-stopping desserts aren't on menus these days. In our recipe, the lemony pound cake is super moist and delicious, and the irresistible Ginger Pastry Cream is the perfect complement for sweet summer strawberries.

MAKE THE LEMON POUND CAKE

1. Preheat the oven to 350°F. Butter a 9 x 5-inch loaf pan.

2. In a medium bowl, beat together the eggs, sugar and vegetable oil until well combined. Stir in the sour cream and lemon zest and mix well.

3. In a medium bowl, sift together the flour and baking soda. Slowly add the flour mixture to the egg mixture, beating just until combined and being careful not to overwork the batter. Pour the batter into the prepared loaf pan and bake until golden brown and a cake tester inserted into the middle of the cake comes out clean, about 1½ hours. Transfer to a rack and let cool in the pan. When cool, remove the cake from the pan and cut into bite-size pieces. The cake can be made a day ahead; allow to cool, cover in plastic wrap and store at room temperature.

PREPARE THE STRAWBERRIES

4. Increase the oven temperature to 375°F. Line a baking sheet with parchment paper.

5. In a large bowl, toss the strawberries with the sugar and vanilla. Spread the strawberries and their juices evenly on the prepared baking sheet and bake until the strawberries are just starting to cook, 7 to 8 minutes. Remove from the oven and allow to cool, keeping any strawberry roasting juices with the strawberries. The strawberries can be prepared ahead and stored in an airtight container for up to 3 days.

MAKE THE GINGER PASTRY CREAM

6. In a medium saucepan, combine the milk, vanilla and ginger and bring to a simmer over low heat.

7. In a large bowl, whisk together the egg yolks, sugar and cornstarch.

8. Gradually whisk the hot milk into the egg mixture. Return it all to the pot and cook over medium heat, whisking constantly, until thickened and glossy, about 2 minutes. Immediately pour the mixture through a strainer into a medium bowl, pressing it through if needed and scraping the pastry cream from the bottom of the strainer. Stir in the butter until melted and smooth. Place a piece of plastic wrap directly on the surface of the custard, let cool to room temperature and then chill completely in the refrigerator. The pastry cream can be made in advance and stored in an airtight container in the refrigerator for up to 3 days.

MAKE THE SWEET CREAM

9. In a large bowl, whisk the cream, icing sugar and vanilla until medium peaks form.

ASSEMBLE THE TRIFLE

10. Layer one-third of the pound cake pieces in the bottom of a large glass bowl or trifle dish. Top with a layer of the ginger pastry cream, then a layer of strawberries with some of their juices. Repeat layers again, reserving some strawberries for garnish. Top with the sweet cream and more strawberries. Keep covered and refrigerated until ready to serve. or up to 3 days.

SERVES 10 TO 12

Lemon Pound Cake (makes 1 loaf)
3 large eggs
1 cup granulated sugar
½ cup vegetable oil
1 cup sour cream
Zest of 2 lemons
1½ cups all-purpose flour
2 teaspoons baking soda

Strawberries
2 pounds (900 g) fresh strawberries, hulled and cut in half
½ cup granulated sugar
1 teaspoon vanilla extract

Ginger Pastry Cream
2 cups whole milk
4 teaspoons vanilla extract
1 tablespoon grated peeled fresh ginger
6 egg yolks
¼ cup granulated sugar
3 tablespoons cornstarch
4 tablespoons unsalted butter

Sweet Cream
1 cup heavy (35%) cream
2 tablespoons icing sugar
½ teaspoon vanilla extract

Ice Cream Three Ways

Nothing screams fun like ice cream. At our house, we celebrate every day with ice cream.

At your next ice cream celebration, we suggest making these three must-have flavours and creating your own ultimate make-your-own ice cream sundae bar with toppings and sauces. Try our Salted Caramel Sauce (page 212), Strawberry Sauce (page 220), Chocolate Sauce (page 221), and Vanilla Whipped Cream (page 221).

EACH RECIPE MAKES 4 CUPS

Vanilla Ice Cream

1. In a large saucepan, combine the cream, milk, sugar, vanilla and salt and bring just to a boil over medium-high heat.
2. In a large bowl, whisk together the egg yolks. Whisking constantly, gradually pour the hot cream mixture in a slow and steady stream into the egg yolks.
3. Scrape the egg yolk mixture back into the saucepan. Cook over low heat, stirring constantly and scraping the bottom with a heatproof rubber spatula, until the custard is thick enough to coat the spatula. Pour the custard through a fine-mesh sieve into a medium bowl, cover the surface with plastic wrap and let cool completely. Refrigerate until chilled, at least 2 hours.
4. Pour the chilled custard into an ice-cream maker and process according to the manufacturer's instructions. Transfer to an airtight container and freeze until set, at least 4 hours. The ice cream can be stored in the freezer for up to 1 week.

2 cups heavy (35%) cream
1 cup whole milk
1 cup granulated sugar
1 tablespoon vanilla paste or vanilla extract
¼ teaspoon kosher salt
5 egg yolks

Salted Caramel Ice Cream

1. In a large saucepan, combine the milk, cream, brown sugar and salt and bring just to a boil over medium-high heat.
2. In a large bowl, whisk together the egg yolks. Whisking constantly, gradually pour the hot cream mixture in a slow and steady stream into the egg yolks. Add the chocolate and stir until the chocolate is melted and combined. Cover the surface with plastic wrap and let cool completely. Refrigerate until chilled, at least 2 hours.
3. Pour the chilled custard into an ice-cream maker and process according to the manufacturer's instructions. Transfer to an airtight container and freeze until set, at least 4 hours. The ice cream can be stored in the freezer for up to 1 week.

1¼ cups whole milk
1¼ cups heavy (35%) cream
¾ cup packed brown sugar
1 teaspoon sea salt
6 egg yolks
2 ounces (57 g) milk chocolate, roughly chopped

Strawberry Ice Cream

1. In a food processor or blender, purée the strawberries with ¼ cup of the sugar. Pour the purée into a measuring cup. You should have about 1½ cups of purée. Keep refrigerated.
2. In a large saucepan, combine the cream, vanilla, salt, and remaining 1 cup sugar and bring just to a boil over medium-high heat.
3. In a large bowl, whisk together the egg yolks. Whisking constantly, gradually pour the hot cream mixture in a slow and steady stream into the egg yolks.
4. Scrape the egg mixture back into the saucepan. Cook over low heat, stirring constantly and scraping the bottom with a heatproof rubber spatula, until the custard is thick enough to coat the spatula. Pour the custard through a fine-mesh sieve into a medium bowl, cover the surface with plastic wrap and let cool completely. Refrigerate until chilled, at least 2 hours.
5. Add the strawberry purée to the chilled custard and stir together. Pour the custard into an ice-cream maker and process according to the manufacturer's instructions. Transfer to an airtight container and freeze until set, at least 4 hours. The ice cream can be stored in the freezer for up to 1 week.

2 pints strawberries (about 1½ pounds), hulled and cut in half
1¼ cups granulated sugar, divided
2½ cups heavy (35%) cream
1 teaspoon vanilla extract
¼ teaspoon kosher salt
2 egg yolks

Strawberry Sauce

The best part about strawberry picking is this strawberry sauce! It is wonderful over pancakes, waffles, cheesecake and of course ice cream. This is our favourite and easiest way to make strawberry sauce.

1. In a medium saucepan, stir together the strawberries, sugar, lemon juice and vanilla until well combined. Cook over medium heat, stirring occasionally, until the strawberries release their juices and the mixture starts to boil, about 5 minutes. Reduce the heat to medium-low and continue to cook, stirring occasionally, until the sauce has thickened, about 10 minutes. Remove from the heat, pour into an airtight container and allow to cool completely. Use immediately or store in the refrigerator for up to 2 weeks.

MAKES ABOUT 1½ CUPS

1 pint fresh strawberries, hulled and sliced
⅓ cup granulated sugar
2 teaspoons lemon juice
1 teaspoon vanilla extract

Chocolate Sauce

This is probably one of the most loved and simplest mixtures around—a satisfying combination of cream and chocolate for any chocolate lover. This is the most decadent sauce for ice cream.

1. In a small saucepan, combine the cream, butter, brown sugar, corn syrup and chocolate chips. Bring to a boil over medium heat. When the mixture is boiling, reduce the heat to low and simmer, stirring continuously, until the chocolate has melted and the sauce is smooth, 3 to 5 minutes. Remove from the heat and stir in the vanilla and salt. Serve immediately or let cool, pour into an airtight container and refrigerate for up to 1 month.

MAKES ABOUT 1 CUP

⅓ cup heavy (35%) cream
3 tablespoons unsalted butter
3 tablespoons brown sugar
3 tablespoons corn syrup
3 ounces (85 g) semisweet chocolate chips
½ teaspoon vanilla extract
Pinch of kosher salt

Vanilla Whipped Cream

Not everyone has a recipe for fresh sweetened homemade whipped cream with only three simple ingredients. Try this one! With its light and billowy texture, it's the perfect topping for pies, cakes, cupcakes, crêpes, cheesecakes, trifles, ice cream and so much more.

1. Using an electric hand mixer, a stand mixer fitted with the whisk attachment or a whisk and a medium bowl, whip the cream, icing sugar and vanilla on medium-high speed until medium peaks form, 3 to 4 minutes. (Peaks will form, but will curl down slightly at the tips.) Serve immediately or store in an airtight container in the refrigerator for up to 2 days.

MAKES ABOUT 1 CUP

1 cup heavy (35%) cream
2 tablespoons icing sugar
½ teaspoon vanilla extract

Sprinkle Cake with Buttercream Frosting

A day without sprinkles is a day without sunshine. Sprinkles are culinary confetti, so it is virtually impossible to be sad when there is sprinkle cake in the room.

Perhaps the most jubilant of all cakes, this scrumptious dessert is a staple in our house. Our daughters absolutely love this enchanting vanilla show-stopper studded with crunchy rainbow-coloured candies inside and out. However, it is not just for the kiddos. Something tells us this will soon become the top cake in your repertoire.

Although we are partial to rainbow sprinkles, you can use other colours (such as chocolate jimmies), confetti style (funfetti) and nonpareils (crunchy round balls).

MAKE THE SPRINKLE CAKE

1. Preheat the oven to 325°F. Butter and flour two 8-inch round cake pans. Line the bottom of the pans with parchment paper.
2. In a medium bowl, whisk together the flour, baking powder, baking soda and salt.
3. In a small bowl, stir together the buttermilk and vanilla.
4. In a stand mixer fitted with the paddle attachment, beat together the butter and sugar at medium-high speed until light and fluffy, 2 to 3 minutes. Reduce the speed to low and, with the mixer running, slowly add the whole eggs and egg yolks, one at a time, beating after each addition, until smooth and creamy, 1 to 2 minutes. Scrape down the bowl. Add the vegetable oil and beat to blend. Add half of the flour mixture, then the milk mixture, then the remaining flour mixture, beating to blend after each addition. Scrape down the bowl and blend once more. Remove the bowl from the mixer and use a spatula or spoon to mix in 3 tablespoons of the sprinkles.
5. Divide the batter evenly between the prepared pans, smooth the tops and bake until the tops are just dry to the touch and a cake tester inserted into the middle of the cakes comes out clean, 20 to 25 minutes. Transfer to a rack and cool the cakes in the pans for 5 to 7 minutes, then turn them out onto racks to cool completely.

MAKE THE BUTTERCREAM FROSTING

6. In a stand mixer fitted with the paddle attachment, cream the butter until light and fluffy. Add the icing sugar, milk and vanilla. Mix on low speed until thickened, 1 to 2 minutes. Add 2 drops of the food colouring and mix until fully incorporated, adding more food colouring if needed to achieve desired colour.

ASSEMBLE THE CAKE

7. Place 1 cake layer bottom side down, on a cake turntable or cake plate. Spread about a quarter of the frosting over the cake. Place the next cake layer, bottom side up, on the filling. Spread the remaining frosting over the top and sides of the cake. Garnish the sides of the cake with the remaining rainbow sprinkles. Chill the cake in the refrigerator for about 1 hour to set before serving. The cake can be stored, covered, in the refrigerator for up to 2 days.

SERVES 12

Sprinkle Cake
3¼ cups all-purpose flour
1 tablespoon baking powder
1½ teaspoons baking soda
1 teaspoon kosher salt
1¼ cups buttermilk, at room temperature
1 teaspoon vanilla extract (or seeds scraped from 1 vanilla bean)
1 cup unsalted butter (2 sticks), at room temperature
2 cups granulated sugar
3 large eggs, at room temperature
3 egg yolks, at room temperature
3 tablespoons vegetable oil
1 cup rainbow sprinkles, divided

Buttercream Frosting
1 cup (2 sticks) unsalted butter, at room temperature
4 cups icing sugar, sifted
4 tablespoons whole milk
2 teaspoons vanilla extract
2 to 4 drops purple food colouring

THE PANTRY

OUR HOME PANTRY

Behind the doors of your cupboards, fridge and freezer lies a powerful range of ingredients that can instantly transform meals, taking them from fine to phenomenal.

From condiments and sauces to vinegars and oils, to preserves and chutneys, to spices, seasonings and marinades, these powerful ingredients are key for building layers of flavour and amping up dishes, resulting in irresistible, scrumptious recipes your whole family will love.

Perhaps the biggest difference between our home pantry and yours is that we make our own stocks, sauces, condiments, spice blends, dressings, marinades and flavour boosters.

In this section, we share a few of our pantry recipes to help you prepare outstanding-tasting food using some of the tricks we have learned over many years of cooking. Here you'll find our favourites, along with many that appear in recipes throughout the book, that we always stock in our kitchen.

Now you will be able to stock your shelves and fridge with bottles, jars and containers filled with bright hits of acid, delicious heat, salty sauces and robust umami flavours that will take your cooking to the next level. It is important to use sterilized jars to store your homemade pantry staples.

SPICE BLENDS

Cajun Spice

Our version of the alluring southern spice gets its heat from cayenne pepper but is not overly hot. So go ahead and use liberally on everything from eggs to roast potatoes to chicken thighs to pork belly.

Featured in: Creole Shrimp and Grits with Sweet Corn Maque Choux (page 79)

1. In a small bowl, whisk together the ingredients until well combined. Store in an airtight container for up to 6 months.

MAKES ABOUT ½ CUP

2 tablespoons smoked paprika
2 tablespoons ground black pepper
1 tablespoon kosher salt
2 teaspoons dried oregano
2 teaspoons dried thyme
2 teaspoons brown sugar
1 teaspoon cayenne pepper

Dukkah Spice

Make room for this nutty spice blend from Egypt. Dukkah can be used to bring flavour and texture to roasted vegetables, stews and salads. When mixed with lemon juice and fresh herbs, the diverse blend becomes a great meat, poultry or fish seasoning, or combine with yogurt to create a tangy, savoury dip.

Featured in: Dukkah Trout with Hummus and Tomato Mint Chutney (page 76)

1. Heat a large, heavy skillet over medium heat. When the skillet is hot, add the nuts and toast, stirring frequently, until fragrant, about 3 minutes. Add the sesame seeds and continue to cook, stirring often, until the sesame seeds start to turn golden brown, about 2 minutes. Transfer the mixture to a food processor.
2. Add the coriander, cumin, allspice, salt and pepper. Pulse until the nuts are broken down and resemble coarse sand. Store in an airtight container for up to 1 month.

MAKES 1 CUP

1 cup assorted raw nuts, such as hazelnuts, almonds, pistachios, cashews, pine nuts
¼ cup sesame seeds
1 teaspoon ground coriander
1 teaspoon ground cumin
⅛ teaspoon ground allspice
1 teaspoon sea salt
½ teaspoon ground black pepper

Five-Spice Powder

This blend of five spices, extensively used in Chinese cuisine, brings warm, spicy-sweet flavours to stir-fries and roasted meats, as well as spice cakes and cookies.

Featured in: Five-Spice Duck Breast with Red Wine Cherry Pan Sauce (page 46), Hoisin Sauce (page 239)

1. Heat a large, heavy skillet over medium heat. When the pan is hot, toast the star anise, peppercorns and fennel seeds, swirling the pan gently and tossing the spices occasionally, until fragrant and slightly toasted, 1 to 2 minutes.
2. Transfer the mixture to a spice grinder. Add the cinnamon and cloves, and grind to a fine powder. Store in an airtight container for up to 6 months.

MAKES ¼ CUP

4 star anise
2 teaspoons Szechuan peppercorns (or 1 tablespoon black peppercorns)
1 tablespoon fennel seeds
1½ teaspoons ground cloves
2 tablespoons cinnamon

Garam Masala

Garam masala is a spice blend widely used in Indian cuisine. There is no single garam masala recipe. The ingredients differ according to the region as well as each chef's preferences. This is our own blend of warming spices. We use it on everything from curries to lentil dishes to soups, and we even sprinkle it on homemade naan and potato chips.

Featured in: Carrot Vindaloo with Raita and Green Chutney (page 8), Tandoori Chicken Naan Pizza (page 53)

1. Heat a large, heavy skillet over medium heat. When the skillet is hot, add the chilies, star anise, cinnamon stick, coriander seeds, fennel seeds, black peppercorns, cardamom pods, ground cloves and cumin seeds, reduce the heat to low and dry-roast the mixture, shaking the pan occasionally, until lightly toasted, 2 to 3 minutes. Spread the spice mixture on a baking sheet to cool.
2. Transfer the mixture to a spice grinder. Add the nutmeg and mace and grind to a fine powder. Store in an airtight container for up to 6 months.

MAKES ABOUT ½ CUP

4 dried Kashmiri chilies
2 star anise
1 cinnamon stick, broken into pieces
2 tablespoons coriander seeds
2 tablespoons fennel seeds
2 tablespoons black peppercorns
1 tablespoon green cardamom pods
2 teaspoons ground cloves
1 teaspoon cumin seeds
¼ teaspoon freshly grated nutmeg
⅛ teaspoon ground mace

Hearth Barbecue Spice Rub

This fragrant, sweet, gently spicy dry rub is all you will need for your barbecue cravings. Outstanding on ribs, burgers and our favourite Sunday roast chicken.

Featured in: Hearth Roasted Chicken (page 61), Oven-Braised Barbecue Beef Brisket with Caramelized Onion Jus (page 91)

1. Heat a large, heavy skillet over medium heat. When the skillet is hot, add the fennel seeds, coriander seeds, cumin seeds and peppercorns and toast, shaking the pan, until the spices release an aroma, 2 to 3 minutes. Tip the toasted spices into a small bowl and let cool.
2. Transfer the toasted spices to a spice grinder and grind to a rough powder. Return the spice powder to the bowl and add the brown sugar, salt, paprika, garlic powder, oregano and cayenne. Stir well. Store in an airtight container for up to 1 week.

MAKES ABOUT 1 CUP

1 tablespoon fennel seeds
1 teaspoon coriander seeds
1 teaspoon cumin seeds
1 teaspoon black peppercorns
½ cup packed brown sugar
⅓ cup sea salt
2 tablespoons smoked paprika
1 tablespoon garlic powder
1 teaspoon dried oregano
1 teaspoon cayenne

My Old Bay Seasoning

Our take on America's best-known spice blend has inspired dozens of recipes for steamed shrimp, seafood, fried chicken, aioli and vodka cocktails. It's one of our go-to seasonings.

Featured in: AP Steak Sauce (page 238), Baked Rigatoni with Meatballs (page 229), Corn, Zucchini and Cheddar Sauté (page 162)

1. In a small bowl, combine the ingredients and stir thoroughly. Store in an airtight container for up to 4 months.

MAKES ¼ CUP

1 tablespoon celery salt
1 teaspoon ground celery seeds
1 teaspoon dry mustard
1 teaspoon ground black pepper
1 teaspoon sweet paprika
1 teaspoon smoked paprika
½ teaspoon ground cloves
½ teaspoon ground ginger
⅛ teaspoon ground allspice
⅛ teaspoon ground cardamom
⅛ teaspoon ground cayenne
⅛ teaspoon ground mace

Ras el Hanout Spice

We adore this aromatic Moroccan spice mix boasting cinnamon, allspice, cumin and ginger. It adds a complex earthiness with a kick to whatever it meets. The warm spices and touch of heat are especially wonderful with fish and seafood.

Featured in: Ras el Hanout Spiced Roast Leg of Lamb with Mint Pomegranate Yogurt (page 99), Moroccan Couscous (page 146)

1. In a small bowl, whisk together the ingredients until well combined. Store in an airtight container for up to 6 months.

MAKES ABOUT ¼ CUP

1 tablespoon ground cumin
1 tablespoon ground ginger
1 tablespoon kosher salt
1 teaspoon freshly ground black pepper
1 teaspoon cinnamon
1 teaspoon ground coriander
½ teaspoon ground allspice
½ teaspoon cayenne
¼ teaspoon ground cloves

Za'atar Spice

Introducing a foolproof formula for creating luscious Middle Eastern fare. With this seasoning mix in hand, you get full-blown flavours with a quick sprinkle and shake, thanks to a wonderful blend of aromatic spices and seeds, including oregano, cumin, sumac, salt and sesame seeds.

Featured in: Fattoush Salad with Heirloom Tomatoes and Za'atar Pita Crisps (page 122), Leek and Spinach Pie (193)

1. In a small bowl, whisk together the ingredients until well combined. Store in an airtight container for up to 3 months.

MAKES ½ CUP

2 tablespoons dried oregano
2 tablespoons toasted sesame seeds
2 tablespoons sumac
2 tablespoons dried thyme
1 tablespoon ground cumin
1 teaspoon kosher salt

FLAVOUR BOOSTERS

Chili Jam

Despite its name, chili jam is not very sweet. In fact, this Asian hot sauce, packed with fiery red chilies and red chili flakes alongside ginger and garlic, is the multi-purpose piquant condiment that boosts everything from a breakfast omelette to a tuna salad sandwich to a roasted leg of lamb.

Featured in: Gai Lan with Chili Jam (page 166)

1. Heat the canola oil and sesame oil in a large nonstick saucepan over medium heat. When the oil is hot, add the chilies, shallots, garlic and ginger. Cook, stirring, until the shallots and garlic begin to caramelize, 2 to 3 minutes.
2. Add the rice wine vinegar, fish sauce, brown sugar and chili flakes. Stir to combine and cook until slightly thickened, 3 to 4 minutes. Allow to cool, then transfer to a jar with a lid and store in the refrigerator for up to 3 weeks.

MAKES ABOUT 1 CUP

2 tablespoons canola or vegetable oil
1 teaspoon sesame oil
½ cup seeded and julienned Fresno chilies
½ cup peeled and julienned shallots
2 cloves garlic, thinly sliced
2 tablespoons roughly chopped peeled fresh ginger
¼ cup rice wine vinegar
1 tablespoon fish sauce
¼ cup packed brown sugar
1 teaspoon red chili flakes

Chili Oil

This chili oil has a magical ability to elevate everything. We like to use it in fried rice, noodles, noodle soups and cold cucumber salads.

Featured in: Dan Dan Noodles (page 31)

1. Heat the canola oil over medium-high heat in a small saucepan. When the oil is hot, add the star anise, cinnamon stick and Szechuan peppercorns. When the oil starts to bubble slightly, reduce the heat to medium or low heat. The oil temperature should be 225°F so the spices do not burn. Let the spices cook in the oil, without stirring, until the seeds and pods are darker in colour, about 20 minutes. Remove from the heat and let the oil cool for 5 minutes.
2. In a medium bowl, combine the chili flakes and salt. Set a fine-mesh sieve over the bowl and pour the oil through the sieve to remove the aromatics. Stir the oil well. When completely cooled, transfer to a jar with a lid and store in the refrigerator for up to 6 months.

MAKES ABOUT 1½ CUPS

1½ cups canola oil
6 star anise
1 cinnamon stick
3 tablespoons Szechuan peppercorns
¾ cup red chili flakes
1 teaspoon sea salt

Crispy Panko Breadcrumbs

While croutons bring a nice crunch to salads, buttery toasted breadcrumbs become the golden crown to casseroles, macaroni and cheese, and baked seafood and pasta dishes.

Featured in: Portobello Mushroom Steaks with Creamed Spinach and Red Wine Shallot Sauce (page 15), Garganelli Pasta with Basil Pesto and Lemon Ricotta (page 36), Bacon and Egg Iceberg Salad with Avocado Dressing (page 113)

1. Melt the butter in a medium skillet over medium-low heat. When the butter is melted and frothy, stir in the panko. Continue stirring until the crumbs are evenly crisp and golden brown. Season with salt and pepper. Remove from the heat and allow to cool. Store in an airtight container at room temperature for up to 2 weeks.

MAKES 1 CUP

3 tablespoons unsalted butter
1 cup panko breadcrumbs
Kosher salt and freshly ground black pepper

Crispy Fried Shallots

Garnish your salads, casseroles, soups and noodle dishes with crispy fried shallots. They will give dishes crunch, golden colour and loads of sweet onion flavour.

Featured in: Singapore Noodles (page 28)

1. Line a plate with paper towel. In a deep medium saucepan, heat 3 inches of canola oil to 375°F.
2. Separate the shallot slices into rings and place them in a medium bowl. Sprinkle cornstarch over the shallots and toss them lightly to coat evenly.
3. Working in small batches, sprinkle the shallots over the hot oil and stir gently to keep them separated. Deep-fry until golden brown, 2 to 3 minutes. Using a slotted spoon, transfer the fried shallots to the paper towel to drain. Sprinkle with salt while still warm. Allow to cool. Store in an airtight container at room temperature for up to 2 weeks.

MAKES ABOUT 2 CUPS

Canola oil, for deep-frying
12 shallots, sliced very thinly crosswise with a mandoline
¼ cup cornstarch
Kosher salt

Furikake Seasoning

This distinct Japanese seasoning of seaweed, dried fish, sesame seeds, salt and sugar adds a crunchy texture to whatever you put it on. Furikake is loaded with umami, making it an ideal pick-me-up for any seafood, rice or vegetable dish.

Featured in: Bacon Okonomiyaki Pancake with Shrimp Tempura (page 71)

1. In a food processor, combine the white and black sesame seeds, nori, bonito flakes, salt, sugar and shichimi togarashi. Pulse just until the mixture is blended. Store in an airtight container for up to 3 months.

MAKES ABOUT ¾ CUP

½ cup toasted white sesame seeds
2 tablespoons black sesame seeds
4 sheets nori, broken
¼ cup packed bonito flakes
2 teaspoons sea salt
1 teaspoon granulated sugar
1 teaspoon shichimi togarashi (Japanese seven spice)

Confit Garlic

Cooking garlic slow and low in oil until it's soft deepens the sweetness and removes the harsh bitterness you will recognize from eating it raw. Cook up a batch bigger than you think you will need, because once you start using it, you will use it with abandon. You can substitute confit garlic for the garlic in any recipe.

Featured in: Baked Rigatoni with Meatballs (page 39), Hearth Roasted Chicken (page 61), Chorizo-Stuffed Cornish Hens with Peperonata and Salsa Verde (page 62), Fogo Island Cod Amandine (page 67), Creole Shrimp and Grits with Sweet Corn Maque Choux (page 79), Cheesy Garlic Pull-Apart Bread (page 149)

MAKES ABOUT 1 CUP

1 cup peeled cloves garlic
½ cup canola oil
½ cup olive oil
½ teaspoon kosher salt

1. Preheat the oven to 300°F.
2. Place the garlic cloves in a heavy medium ovenproof pot. Pour the canola oil and olive oil over the garlic, adding more oil if needed to cover it, then add the salt. Cover, transfer to the oven and bake until the garlic cloves are pale gold and tender, about 50 minutes. Cool to room temperature.
3. Using a slotted spoon, transfer the garlic cloves to a food processor and process until smooth. Alternatively, transfer the cloves to a bowl and mash with the side of a knife. Store in an airtight container in the refrigerator for up to 1 month or freeze for up to 3 months.

Garlic Ginger Paste

This simple but powerful purée of garlic, ginger and miso is the flavour bomb you have been waiting for. Use this in place of garlic or ginger in most recipes.

MAKES ABOUT ½ CUP

¼ cup roughly chopped peeled fresh ginger
¼ cup peeled cloves garlic
1 tablespoon white miso
2 tablespoons canola oil

1. In a small blender, combine the ginger, garlic and miso. Purée, gradually adding enough canola oil to make a smooth paste. Store in an airtight container in the refrigerator for up to 2 weeks or freeze for up to 6 months.

Harissa Paste

You do not have to travel all the way to Tunisia to experience the bold flavours of this hot chili paste. Unlike other spicy purées, this one is not too fiery and delivers a decadent smokiness that you will come to love and rely on.

Featured in: Butternut Squash with Trimmings (page 16), Harissa-Roasted Parsnips with Whipped Feta, Pistachios and Rosemary Honey (page 169); also a great condiment for Moroccan Couscous (page 146)

MAKES ABOUT 1 CUP

4 red bell peppers, roasted, seeded and diced
3 tablespoons extra-virgin olive oil
4 teaspoons Sriracha sauce
1 tablespoon minced garlic
2 teaspoons ground cumin
1 teaspoon ground cardamom
1 teaspoon ground coriander
Kosher salt and freshly ground black pepper

1. In a food processor or blender, combine the bell peppers, olive oil, Sriracha sauce, garlic, cumin, cardamom and coriander. Blend until smooth. Season with salt and pepper. Store in an airtight container in the refrigerator for up to 1 month.

Tamarind Date Paste

A sweet-and-sour chutney of sweet dates balanced by the complex sourness of tamarind.

Featured in: Spaghetti Squash Pad Thai (page 19), Potato Aloo Chaat with Tamarind Chutney, Cilantro Yogurt and Bhel Puri (page 177)

1. In a large saucepan, combine the ingredients and simmer over low heat, stirring frequently, until well blended and thick, about 30 minutes. Remove from the heat and allow to cool.
2. When cooled, remove the thyme sprigs. Purée the chutney in a blender until smooth, adding water to achieve desired consistency. Store in an airtight container in the refrigerator for up to 4 weeks or freeze for up to 6 months.

MAKES ABOUT 1¼ CUPS

½ cup pitted Medjool dates
¼ cup seedless tamarind pulp
¼ cup raisins
¼ cup packed brown sugar
1 tablespoon Kashmiri chili powder
½ teaspoon cinnamon
2 sprigs fresh thyme
Zest and juice of 2 oranges

Jerk Marinade

This distinctive jerk marinade has it all—heat, spice, smokiness, woodiness and sweetness. The combination of Jamaican warm spice, hot peppers and thyme is packed with Caribbean flavour. This is a delicious marinade used on any cut of meat, fish or poultry.

Featured in: Jerk Chicken Curry with Coconut Rice (page 58)

1. Place the ingredients in a blender and purée until a thick paste forms. Store in an airtight container in the refrigerator for up to 2 weeks.

MAKES 1 CUP

¼ cup white vinegar
3 tablespoons olive oil
1 bunch of green onions, coarsely chopped
1 or 2 Scotch bonnet peppers, stem and seeds removed
2 tablespoons brown sugar
2 tablespoons fresh thyme leaves
2 teaspoons ground allspice
2 teaspoons cinnamon
2 teaspoons kosher salt
2 teaspoons freshly ground black pepper
1 teaspoon nutmeg

Steak and Everything Marinade

One of the simplest ways to flavour food is to marinate it. This marinade is perfect on a steak, but also so good in the mushroom steaks recipe.

Featured in: Portobello Mushroom Steaks with Creamed Spinach and Red Wine Shallot Sauce (page 15)

1. In a small bowl, stir together the ingredients. Pour into an airtight container and store in the refrigerator for up to 2 weeks.

MAKES ABOUT 1 CUPS

½ cup soy sauce
⅓ cup olive oil
2 tablespoons Dijon mustard
2 tablespoons Worcestershire sauce
1 large clove garlic, grated

Mushroom Powder

Mushroom powder may quickly become one of your favourite pantry items. It is simple to make and can be used in a variety of ways in your kitchen. Talk about an umami bomb! Earthy, packed with depth of flavour, it does not take much of this power-packed powder to deliver serious results. Dust on everything from soups to salads to pastas to seared meats and all seafood.

Featured in: Mushroom Bolognese Pappardelle (page 32), Chicken Marsala (page 54), Miso Black Cod with Mushroom Soy Broth (Umami Aioli; page 85), Mushroom Risotto (page 145), Mushroom XO Sauce (page 241)

MAKES ABOUT ¼ CUP

2 ounces (57 g) dried mushrooms, such as a mix of porcini, shiitake, portobello

1. In a spice grinder or small food processor, grind the mushrooms to a fine powder. Store in an airtight container at room temperature for up to 3 months.

Rosemary Honey

At our restaurant we used this rosemary-infused honey on everything from our rotating cheeseboard to vegetables like creamy parsnips and roasted carrots to our famous fried chicken.

Featured in: Baked Sweet Potatoes with Chipotle Lime Crema, Pecans and Rosemary Honey (page 137), Harissa-Roasted Parsnips with Whipped Feta, Pistachios and Rosemary Honey (page 169), Roasted Cauliflower with Ricotta Salata and Lemon Caper Rémoulade (page 178)

MAKES 1 CUP

1 cup honey
Peel of 1 lemon, cut into strips
2 sprigs fresh rosemary

1. In a small saucepan over medium-low heat, heat the honey, lemon peel and rosemary until warm to the touch. Transfer the mixture to a mason jar, seal and store at room temperature for up to 1 month.

Lemon Purée

This lemon purée is a must to always have on hand in your fridge. We use this as a substitute for lemon juice and zest to give a refreshing lemon flavour to many of our recipes.

Featured in: Fogo Island Cod Amandine (page 67), Halibut with 'Nduja, Cauliflower, Kale and Toasted Hazelnuts (page 68), Creole Shrimp and Grits with Sweet Corn Maque Choux (page 79), Ras el Hanout Spiced Roast Leg of Lamb with Mint Pomegranate Yogurt (page 99), Pea Shoot and Sweet Pea Sauté with Pancetta and Lemon (page 173)

MAKES ABOUT 1 CUP

3 lemons, thinly sliced and seeds removed
2 cups water
1 cup granulated sugar
½ teaspoon kosher salt
2 tablespoons apple cider vinegar

1. Place the lemon slices in a saucepan and add water to just cover the slices. Add the sugar, salt and apple cider vinegar. Cook over low heat until the lemons are very soft, about 1 hour. Remove from the heat and cool completely.
2. Transfer the slices to a blender and purée, adding some cooking liquid if necessary to make the purée smooth. Store in an airtight container in the refrigerator for up to 1 month.

Orange Purée

This orange purée does not have to be relegated to merely a toast topper. Slather it over chicken before roasting, add a dollop or two to sweet treats or create a sticky glaze, dip or salad dressing.

Featured in: Ras el Hanout Spiced Roast Leg of Lamb with Mint Pomegranate Yogurt (page 99), Honey-Garlic Ribs (page 107)

1. Place the ingredients in a medium saucepan. Cook over low heat until the liquid is reduced by half and the orange slices are very soft, about 1 hour. Remove from the heat and allow to cool slightly.
2. When the mixture is cool, pour it into a blender and blend until smooth. Store in an airtight container in the refrigerator for up to 2 months.

MAKES 1 CUP

2 oranges, thinly sliced and seeds
   removed
2 cups water
1½ cups granulated sugar

Pickled Jalapeños

These fiery little peppers are tamed down a bit in this vibrant pickling liquid. We use them in salads, dressings, sandwiches and tacos.

1. Place the sliced jalapeños in a 2-cup mason jar.
2. In a small saucepan, combine the garlic, water, apple cider vinegar, mustard seeds, sugar, salt and bay leaf. Bring to a boil, stirring occasionally to dissolve the sugar and salt. Once the liquid comes to a boil, pour over the jalapeños. Allow to cool, then seal the jar with a lid and store in the refrigerator for up to 2 months.

MAKES 2 CUPS

5 jalapeño peppers, thinly sliced
2 cloves garlic, peeled
½ cup water
½ cup apple cider vinegar
1 tablespoon yellow mustard seeds
1 tablespoon granulated sugar
2 teaspoons kosher salt
1 bay leaf

Pickled Mustard Seeds

These versatile, tangy little seeds will brighten up any dish and add texture with subtle caviar-like mustard explosions in your mouth. A tasty addition to egg salad, tuna salad, green salads, sauces, a charcuterie board or a perfectly grilled steak.

1. Place the mustard seeds in a small saucepan, cover with cold water and bring to a boil. When the water is boiling, strain the mustard seeds through a fine-mesh sieve. Repeat this process 3 more times, using fresh water each time.
2. In the same saucepan, combine 1 cup cold water with the apple cider vinegar, sugar, salt and the blanched mustard seeds. Bring to a boil, then pour into a jar. Allow to cool, then seal the jar with a lid and store in the refrigerator for up to 2 months.

MAKES ABOUT 1 CUP

¼ cup yellow mustard seeds
½ cup apple cider vinegar
1½ teaspoons granulated sugar
½ teaspoon kosher salt

STOCKS, SAUCES, CONDIMENTS AND DRESSINGS

Roasted Chicken Stock

Roasting the chicken before adding it to the stock elevates the depth and adds a hint of richness. We reduce this down and use for all our poultry and meat recipes.

1. Preheat the oven to 425°F.
2. Spread the chicken bones in a large roasting pan. Drizzle with the canola oil and toss well to coat. Roast, uncovered, until golden brown, about 45 minutes, turning several times during roasting. Transfer the chicken bones to a stockpot and set aside.
3. To the roasting pan, add the leeks, onions, celery, carrots and garlic. Return the pan to the oven and roast the vegetables for about 20 minutes, tossing several times during roasting.
4. Remove the pan from the oven and set it over medium heat on the stovetop. Stir in 1 cup water and deglaze the pan, using a wooden spoon to scrape up any brown bits stuck to the bottom. Stir in the tomato paste and cook, stirring frequently, for 5 minutes. Transfer the vegetables and roasting juices to the chicken bones in the stockpot and add just enough cold water to cover. Stir in the parsley, thyme sprigs, bay leaves and peppercorns. Bring to a boil over medium-high heat. Reduce the heat to low and simmer, uncovered and without stirring, for 2 hours, skimming impurities from the surface as the stock cooks down.
5. Strain the stock through a fine-mesh sieve into a container. Discard the solids. Set the container in a kitchen sink surrounded by ice water to cool as quickly as possible. Store the cooled stock covered in the refrigerator for up to 1 week or freeze for up to 3 months.

MAKES ABOUT 2 QUARTS

4 pounds (1.8 kg) chicken bones (wings, backs and necks)
3 tablespoons canola oil
2 leeks (white and light green parts only), cut crosswise into thirds
3 white onions, cut in half crosswise
4 stalks celery, cut crosswise into thirds
3 carrots, quartered
1 whole head of garlic, cut in half crosswise
1 cup water
2 tablespoons tomato paste
½ bunch of fresh flat-leaf parsley
5 sprigs fresh thyme
2 bay leaves
½ teaspoon black peppercorns

Fish Stock

This fish stock is the perfect foundation for chowders, soups, seafood stews and fish sauces.

1. Melt the butter in a stockpot over medium-high heat. Add the celery, onion, leek, fennel, peppercorns, fennel seeds, bay leaves, thyme and parsley. Sauté, stirring frequently, until the vegetables are soft, about 5 minutes. Add the white wine and continue cooking until the liquid has reduced by half. Add the fish bones and just enough cold water to cover them. Bring to a boil. Reduce the heat to low and simmer, uncovered, for 20 minutes, skimming impurities from the surface as the stock cooks down.
2. Stir in the chervil and salt and simmer the stock for 10 minutes more. Strain the stock through a fine-mesh sieve into a container. Discard the solids. Set the container in a kitchen sink surrounded by ice water to cool as quickly as possibile. Store the cooled stock covered in the refrigerator for up to 2 days or freeze for up to 3 months.

MAKES 2 QUARTS

2 tablespoons unsalted butter
2 stalks celery, cut into 1-inch pieces
1 onion, quartered
1 leek (white part only), thinly sliced
½ bulb fennel, thinly sliced
½ teaspoon white peppercorns
6 fennel seeds
2 bay leaves
2 sprigs fresh thyme
8 sprigs fresh flat-leaf parsley
1 cup dry white wine
2 pounds (900 g) white fish bones, rinsed clean in cold water, cut into 2-inch pieces
¼ bunch of fresh chervil, stems only
2 teaspoons kosher salt

Vegetable Stock

Every time we make vegetable stock, we wonder why people ever bother buying it in the store. It is so easy! Chop up some vegetables, cover with water, and simmer. You will have enough stock to make your soups, casseroles, and pilafs for weeks to come, and all in just a little over an hour.

1. Place the carrots, celery, leeks, onions and mushrooms in a stockpot. Add enough water to cover the vegetables and bring to a boil over medium-high heat.
2. Reduce the heat to low and simmer for 10 minutes. Add the parsley, thyme, star anise, peppercorns and fennel seeds and simmer for another 5 minutes. Remove from the heat and stir in the lemon slices.
3. Strain the stock through a fine-mesh sieve into a large container. Discard the solids. Set the container in a kitchen sink surrounded by ice water to cool as quickly as possible. Store the cooled stock covered in the refrigerator for up to 1 week or freeze for up to 3 months.

MAKES ABOUT 8 CUPS

6 carrots, cut into 1-inch rounds
4 stalks celery, thinly sliced
2 leeks (white part only), thinly sliced
3 white onions, thinly sliced
2 cups mushrooms or mushroom stems
6 sprigs fresh flat-leaf parsley
4 sprigs fresh thyme
1 star anise
5 white peppercorns
1 teaspoon fennel seeds
½ lemon, sliced

AP Steak Sauce

As much as we love the classics, our version of this versatile sauce is less sweet, more complex, and yet takes just minutes to make using simple ingredients. Why is it called AP Steak Sauce? Because our daughter Addie Pepper loves it! Win-win. This is a great sauce for everything that comes off the barbecue, and is perfect with grilled chicken, roast beef or sautéed shrimp.

Featured in: Asado Grilled Flank Steak with Steak Sauces (page 96)

1. In a medium saucepan, heat the olive oil over medium heat. Add the onion and garlic and cook, stirring occasionally, until the onion is softened, about 5 minutes. Add the honey, brown sugar, gochujang, paprika and Old Bay seasoning and cook, stirring, until the gochujang deepens in colour, about 1 minute. Add the orange zest and juice, balsamic vinegar, ketchup, Worcestershire sauce, mustard, soy sauce and water. Simmer over medium heat, stirring occasionally, until thickened slightly, about 30 minutes.
2. Season with salt and pepper. Scrape the sauce into a blender; let cool slightly. Purée the sauce until very smooth, about 2 minutes. Let cool to room temperature before serving. Store in an airtight container in the refrigerator for up to 2 weeks.

MAKES ABOUT 2 CUPS

3 tablespoons olive oil
1 white onion, finely chopped
2 cloves garlic, finely chopped
2 tablespoons honey
1 tablespoon brown sugar
1 tablespoon gochujang
1 teaspoon smoked paprika
1 teaspoon My Old Bay Seasoning (page 229 or store-bought)
Zest and juice of 1 orange
¼ cup balsamic vinegar
¼ cup ketchup
3 tablespoons Worcestershire sauce
2 tablespoons Dijon mustard
2 tablespoons soy sauce
½ cup water
Kosher salt and freshly ground black pepper

Chimichurri Sauce

This bright, herbaceous Argentinean sauce packs a garlicky punch boosted with parsley, mixed in with a hit of acid, thanks to rice vinegar. We use it with our flank steak recipe, but it is also great on our Hearth Roasted Chicken (page 61).

Featured in: Asado Grilled Flank Steak with Steak Sauces (page 96)

1. In a medium bowl, combine the ingredients. Store in an airtight container for up to 1 week.

MAKES ABOUT 2 CUPS

1 cup packed fresh cilantro, chopped
½ cup packed fresh flat-leaf parsley, chopped
2 tablespoons chopped fresh oregano
4 green onions, chopped
1 jalapeño pepper, seeded and finely chopped
1 to 2 cloves garlic, finely minced
½ cup extra-virgin olive oil
¼ cup unseasoned rice vinegar
Juice of 1 lime

Hoisin Sauce

This homemade version is seasoned with soy, peanut butter and miso. It's salty, nutty, slightly sweet and spiced.

Featured in: Dan Dan Noodles (page 31), Five-Spice Duck Breast with Red Wine Cherry Pan Sauce (page 46), Honey-Garlic Ribs (page 107), Blistered Beans with Ginger, Black Garlic and Cashews (page 154), Gai Lan with Chili Jam (page 166), Hoisin-Glazed Eggplant with Sesame Miso Baba Ganoush (page 170)

1. In a medium saucepan, combine the soy sauce, brown sugar, peanut butter, miso, rice wine vinegar, lemon juice, garlic, sambal oelek, and five-spice powder. Cook over low heat, stirring frequently, until smooth, about 5 minutes. Bring to a boil, then reduce the heat and simmer until the sauce has thickened slightly. Remove from the heat and stir in the sesame oil. Allow to cool, then store in a sealed jar in the refrigerator for up to 1 month.

MAKES ABOUT 1 CUP

¼ cup soy sauce
2 tablespoons brown sugar
2 tablespoons peanut butter
2 tablespoons miso
2 tablespoons rice wine vinegar
1 teaspoon lemon juice
1 teaspoon minced garlic
1 teaspoon sambal oelek
½ teaspoon Five-Spice Powder (page 228 or store-bought)
½ teaspoon sesame oil

House Hot Sauce

Many store-bought hot sauces err on the side of either sweat-inducing heat or lack of body. This homemade concoction delivers serious flavour with an enticing kick. In our family, we all use it and we put it on everything! From jazzing up our morning scrambled eggs to adding it to melted brown butter to spice up popcorn on movie night, it's one of the most versatile and tastiest condiments we know.

MAKES ABOUT 1 CUP

2 tablespoons olive oil
1 white onion, finely diced
4 cloves garlic, peeled
2 Thai chilies (or use your favourite hot chili, to taste)
2 tablespoons brown sugar
2 teaspoons smoked paprika
1 jar (10 ounces/300 mL) roasted red peppers, drained
2 tomatoes, roughly chopped
½ cup apple cider vinegar
Zest and juice of l lemon
Kosher salt

1. Heat the olive oil in a large saucepan over medium heat. Add the onion, garlic and chilies and cook, stirring frequently, until the onions are softened, 4 to 5 minutes.
2. Add the brown sugar, paprika, roasted peppers and tomatoes and continue to cook for 20 minutes, stirring until the liquid has evaporated.
3. Add the apple cider vinegar and lemon zest and juice, and season with salt. Cook, stirring frequently, for 5 minutes.
4. Transfer to a high-speed blender and blend until smooth. Strain into a jar and allow to cool. Store, covered, in the refrigerator for up to 1 month.

Lynn and Lora's Barbecue Sauce

An outstanding barbecue sauce requires a good balance of sweet and heat. This finger-lickin' recipe has been our go-to since our early cooking days and has stood the test of time and many cottage meals. It's great on ribs, burgers and chicken wings.

MAKES 4 CUPS

2 tablespoons canola oil
2 white onions, finely chopped
3 cloves garlic, grated
2 cups crushed tomatoes
1 cup ketchup
¼ cup maple syrup
2 tablespoons apple cider vinegar
2 tablespoons tomato paste
2 tablespoons Dijon mustard
2 chipotle peppers in adobo sauce, minced
Salt and freshly ground black pepper

1. In a medium saucepan, heat the canola oil over medium heat. Add the onions and garlic and cook, stirring frequently, until the onions are soft and translucent, about 5 minutes.
2. Stir in the tomatoes, ketchup, maple syrup, apple cider vinegar, tomato paste, mustard and chipotle peppers. Reduce the heat to medium-low and simmer, uncovered and stirring occasionally, until reduced by one-quarter, about 45 minutes.
3. Working in batches, purée the sauce in a blender. Season with salt and pepper. Store in an airtight container in the refrigerator for up to 1 month.

Mushroom XO Sauce

The iconic condiment XO sauce, hailing from Hong Kong, is made with some powerful ingredients like dried shrimp, dried scallops and Jinhua ham. Our vegetarian version is packed with a meaty, rich shiitake mushroom base that makes this XO just as iconic to us. A wonderful condiment for fish, chicken and pasta.

Featured in: Mongolian Beef Stir-Fry with Mushroom XO Sauce (page 95)

1. In a small bowl, combine the soy sauce, rice vinegar and brown sugar, stirring to dissolve the sugar.
2. In a large skillet, heat the olive oil over medium heat. Add the mushrooms and cook, stirring frequently, until golden brown, about 5 minutes. Add the shallots, garlic, ginger and chili and cook, stirring occasionally, until softened, about 4 minutes. Add the fermented black beans, chili sauce and the soy sauce mixture and continue to cook for 2 minutes to reduce the liquid. Add the sesame oil, green onions and mushroom powder, season with salt and pepper, and cook for another minute. Remove from the heat and allow to cool. Store in an airtight container in the refrigerator for up to 2 weeks.

MAKES ABOUT 1½ CUPS

¼ cup soy sauce
3 tablespoons unseasoned rice vinegar
2 tablespoons brown sugar
2 tablespoons olive oil
7 ounces (200 g) shiitake mushrooms, stems removed, finely chopped
2 shallots, finely diced
3 cloves garlic, minced
1 (½-inch) piece fresh ginger, peeled and diced
1 Fresno chili, thinly sliced
1 tablespoon fermented black beans, rinsed and mashed
2 teaspoons chili sauce, such as sambal oelek
1 teaspoon sesame oil
2 green onions, finely chopped
1 tablespoon Mushroom Powder (page 235)
Kosher salt and freshly ground black pepper

Ponzu Sauce

Our take on a classic Japanese dipping sauce marries citrus and bonito, a smoked dried tuna. It makes an amazing marinade or base for dressings.

1. In a medium bowl, combine the soy sauce, rice vinegar, water, mirin, bonito and brown sugar. Whisk until the sugar dissolves.
2. Add the garlic and squeeze the lemons and orange into the mixture, then add the juiced halves to the bowl as well. Transfer the sauce to an airtight container and store in the refrigerator for up to 2 days. Strain the sauce, discarding the solids. Store in the refrigerator for up to 1 month.

MAKES ABOUT 1 CUP

½ cup soy sauce
¼ cup seasoned rice vinegar
¼ cup water
3 tablespoons mirin
¼ cup bonito flakes
1 tablespoon brown sugar
2 cloves garlic, cut in half lengthwise
2 large lemons, cut in half
1 orange, cut in half

Spicy Ginger Lime Mayonnaise

You will notice in our recipes that we love a kick of spice. We use this mayo for everything from dipping roast chicken in to drizzling over crisp green beans.

Featured in: Maui Fried Chicken (page 57), Bacon Okonomiyaki Pancake with Shrimp Tempura (page 71)

1. In a small bowl, whisk together the ingredients until combined. Store in an airtight container in the refrigerator for up to 2 weeks.

MAKES ABOUT ½ CUP

½ cup mayonnaise
2 tablespoons sambal oelek
1 teaspoon lime juice
2 tablespoons chopped fresh cilantro
2 teaspoons grated peeled fresh ginger

Preserved Lemon Slices

Preserved lemons have always been a staple in our kitchen. They do take a bit of time but they are well worth it. They add a wonderful burst of citrus to everything from dressings and salads to vegetables, stews and pasta dishes.

Featured in: Fogo Island Cod Amandine (page 67)

1. In a medium bowl, combine the lemon slices, salt, sugar, honey and chili flakes, if using. Cover with plastic wrap and set aside in a cool, dark place for 3 days.
2. Transfer the lemon mixture to a mason jar, add olive oil and seal with a lid. Refrigerate for 3 weeks, occasionally shaking the jar to distribute the flavours. Store in the refrigerator for up to 2 months.

MAKES ABOUT 2 CUPS

6 lemons, cut into ¼-inch slices
¼ cup kosher salt
¼ cup granulated sugar
¼ cup honey
¼ teaspoon red chili flakes (optional)
2 tablespoons olive oil

Green Chutney

This chutney adds a bright, fresh finish to our carrot vindaloo. We bring out this chutney whenever we fire up the barbecue. It is the perfect condiment for a mixed grill of lamb, chicken, sausages and veggies.

Featured in: Carrot Vindaloo with Raita and Green Chutney (page 8)

1. In a blender, combine the yogurt, lime juice, honey, chili, cilantro and mint. Blend until smooth, adding more yogurt if needed. Season with salt and pepper. Scrape into a bowl. Cover and refrigerate for up to 2 days.

MAKES ABOUT 1½ CUPS

¾ cup plain full-fat Greek yogurt
1 teaspoon lime juice
1 teaspoon honey
½ to 1 small green chili, stem and seeds removed
2 cups fresh cilantro, leaves and stems, chopped
1 cup fresh mint leaves
Kosher salt and freshly ground black pepper

Tomato Chutney

The key to this spectacular spread is to use fresh tomatoes, not canned ones. Cooked down slowly into a jammy consistency, this sweet and savoury condiment will be your new favourite go-to. We use it on everything from eggs to burgers to pizza to rice.

MAKES 2 CUPS

2 tablespoons canola oil
2 shallots, thinly sliced
2 cloves garlic, thinly sliced
2 teaspoons grated peeled fresh ginger
1 tablespoon tomato paste
1 cup tomato purée
2 medium tomatoes, diced
½ cup sun-dried tomatoes, thinly sliced
3 tablespoons apple cider vinegar
2 tablespoons brown sugar
1 cup cherry tomatoes, cut in half
½ cup fresh basil leaves, roughly chopped
Kosher salt and freshly ground black pepper

1. In a medium saucepan, heat the canola oil over medium heat. Add the shallots, garlic and ginger and cook, stirring occasionally, until softened and just starting to brown, about 5 minutes.
2. Add the tomato paste and cook, stirring, until the vegetables are evenly coated, about 1 minute. Add the tomato purée, diced tomatoes, sun-dried tomatoes, apple cider vinegar and brown sugar. Bring to a boil over high heat, then reduce the heat and simmer, stirring frequently, until thickened, about 15 minutes. Remove from the heat and stir in the cherry tomatoes and basil. Let cool. Season the chutney with salt and pepper. Transfer to an airtight container and store in the refrigerator for up to 1 month.

Pepper and Aubergine Relish

Named after our two daughters, Addie Pepper and Gemma Jet Aubergine, this chunky antipasto of peppers and eggplant is the perfect accompaniment for pretty much everything: steak, rice and especially pita chips.

MAKES ABOUT 2 CUPS

2 large red bell peppers (or one 12-ounce/370 mL jar roasted red peppers, diced)
½ cup olive oil, divided
2 medium globe or Italian eggplants, cut into ½-inch dice (about 4 cups), divided
Kosher salt and freshly ground black pepper
¼ cup raisins
2 tablespoons sherry vinegar
2 tablespoons balsamic vinegar
2 tablespoons honey
1 tablespoon grated peeled fresh ginger
1 tablespoon brown sugar
1 sprig fresh thyme

1. To roast the bell peppers, place them directly on a gas burner, under a hot broiler or on a hot charcoal or gas grill. Keep rotating the peppers until evenly charred all over. Transfer to a small bowl, cover tightly with plastic wrap and let cool.
2. Peel the peppers over the same bowl to catch any juice. Discard the skin. Split the peppers over the bowl and remove and discard the stem and as many of the seeds as possible. Set the juice aside. Dice the peppers and place in a medium bowl. Strain the pepper juice over the diced peppers.
3. In a large skillet over high heat, combine ¼ cup of the olive oil and half (about 2 cups) of the diced eggplant. Season the eggplant well with salt and pepper and cook, stirring frequently, until it is caramelized, 4 to 5 minutes. Transfer the eggplant to a plate. Repeat with the remaining eggplant and the remaining ¼ cup olive oil.
4. Return the skillet to medium heat and add the raisins, sherry vinegar, balsamic vinegar, honey, ginger, brown sugar and thyme. Bring to a boil. Add the roasted peppers with their juices and the eggplant. Cook, stirring frequently, until the relish has thickened and most of the liquid has evaporated, 10 to 15 minutes. Remove from the heat and allow to cool. Store in mason jars in the refrigerator for up to 3 months.

Olive Tapenade

Whether you use Greek Kalamata, Castelvetrano or Cerignola from Italy, Niçoise from France or Chilean Alfonsos, blitzing them up with capers, anchovies, garlic, parsley, olive oil and lemon juice results in a salty, briny explosion that's as good smothered across toast as it is mixed into pasta.

1. In a small food processor, combine the garlic, olives, capers, anchovies, parsley, lemon juice and olive oil. Process until everything is finely chopped. Season with salt and pepper. Store in an airtight container in the refrigerator for up to 1 month.

MAKES ABOUT 1½ CUPS

3 cloves garlic, finely chopped
1 cup pitted olives
2 tablespoons drained capers
2 anchovy fillets
3 tablespoons chopped fresh flat-leaf parsley
2 tablespoons lemon juice
2 tablespoons olive oil
Kosher salt and freshly ground black pepper

Kimchi

Kimchi has a distinctive taste, a spicy, earthy flavour of fermented vegetables. Traditionally, kimchi is left to ferment for weeks, months or even years. Our version is a lot quicker! Cabbage, ginger, apple, chilies and green onions are pickled in a soy sauce brine, ready to enjoy the next day.

Featured in: Korean Barbecue Tofu Lettuce Wraps (page 12)

1. To a large pot of boiling salted water, add the cabbage and blanch for 1 minute. Drain the cabbage and transfer to an ice bath to stop the cooking. Drain well. Place in a large bowl with the carrot and apple.
2. In a saucepan, combine the rice vinegar, sugar and salt. Bring to a simmer over medium heat and cook until the sugar dissolves. Add the garlic, green onions, chili and ginger and cook for 1 minute more. Pour the vinegar mixture over the cabbage mixture. Add the cilantro, soy sauce and sesame oil and fold gently to combine.
3. Transfer the kimchi to a 4-cup mason jar, cover and refrigerate overnight to allow the flavours to meld. Store in the refrigerator for up to 1 month.

MAKES ABOUT 4 CUPS

1 napa cabbage, cut in half lengthwise, cored and cut into 1-inch chunks (about 10 cups)
1 small carrot, peeled and thinly sliced on the diagonal
½ red apple, peeled, cored and cut into matchsticks
1 cup seasoned rice vinegar
2 tablespoons granulated sugar
1 teaspoon kosher salt
4 large cloves garlic, roughly chopped
3 green onions, cut into 1-inch pieces
½ Fresno chili, thinly sliced
5 thin slices peeled fresh ginger
½ cup roughly chopped cilantro
3 tablespoons soy sauce
1 teaspoon sesame oil

Lemon Caper Rémoulade

This rémoulade is the perfect sauce for your fancy French seafood dishes, but do not stop there. Our kids love this condiment on burgers and fries, and it is perfect in a sandwich with leftover Grilled Mojo Chicken (page 45).

Featured in: Lobster Potato Salad (page 126), Roasted Cauliflower with Ricotta Salata and Lemon Caper Rémoulade (page 178)

1. In a small bowl, whisk together the ingredients. Store in an airtight container in the refrigerator for up to 2 weeks.

MAKES ABOUT 1¼ CUPS

1 cup mayonnaise
2 tablespoons minced drained capers
2 tablespoons chopped cornichons
1 tablespoon chopped fresh dill
1 tablespoon chopped fresh flat-leaf parsley
Zest and juice of 2 lemons
Kosher salt and freshly ground black pepper

Caesar Dressing

Creamy, garlicky, cheesy—the perfect flavour and texture trifecta. We are partial to this essential steakhouse salad dressing in a sandwich, smothered over meat or as a dip for chicken fingers and veggies.

1. In a food processor, combine the egg yolks, mustard, garlic, anchovies and lemon juice. Process until smooth. With the motor running, slowly add the olive oil in a steady stream until the dressing is thick. Add the Parmesan and pulse 3 times to combine. Season with salt and pepper. Store in an airtight container in the refrigerator for up to 1 month.

MAKES 2½ CUPS

2 extra-large egg yolks, at room temperature
2 teaspoons Dijon mustard
2 teaspoons chopped garlic
2 to 4 anchovy fillets
½ cup freshly squeezed lemon juice
1½ cups extra-virgin olive oil
½ cup grated Parmesan cheese
Kosher salt and freshly ground black pepper

Our House Vinaigrette

This is the vinaigrette that we enjoy the most. It has such great depth of flavour and is so easy to whip up.

1. In a medium bowl, whisk together the red wine vinegar, balsamic vinegar, honey, mustard, Worcestershire sauce, salt and lemon juice until well combined. While whisking, slowly drizzle in the canola oil until emulsified. Store in an airtight container in the refrigerator for up to 2 months.

MAKES ABOUT 2 CUPS

½ cup red wine vinegar
2 teaspoons balsamic vinegar
2 tablespoons honey
2 tablespoons Dijon mustard
1 tablespoon Worcestershire sauce
¼ teaspoon kosher salt
Juice of 1 lemon
1⅓ cups canola oil

ACKNOWLEDGEMENTS

It's been an incredible journey to write this book together and we were so lucky to have such a strong, talented team of women with us to make this book happen. We all know that with children it takes a village, so we are thankful for our village and all the support it gave us during this project.

Thank you to our favourite and exceptionally talented editor, Andrea Magyar. You have done it again! We thank you and your amazing team at Penguin Canada for this opportunity to create another wonderful cookbook with you. It is such an incredible gift to work with such a supportive and creative publishing team.

Thank you, Maya Visnyei, whose photographic talent, vision, passion and attention to detail blew us out of the water. A chef could only dream of having their dishes look so good for so many to enjoy. You transformed our dishes into works of art. Your work is stunning, so beautiful and real. It was a pleasure to have had the opportunity to work with you, and we hope to do it again soon!

Thank you, Sasha Seymour. We could go on for days about you and your talented stylist self! We've had the pleasure of working with you on so many projects over the years. You are a constant source of inspiration, positivity, passion and laughs. We so appreciate you and all of your many, many, many talents. You bring so much love and life to so many around you through your love of food, style, taste and design. You brought our book to life in such a beautiful way. Thank you from the bottom of our hearts!

Thank you, Stephanie Dickinson, who rocked it with her writing talents, enthusiasm, energy, positive spirit, love of food, hospitality and bottomless pots of spice tea. You helped us get the best out of our recipes from the conversations we shared together and helped to get them onto these pages.

Thank you to our kitchen team, Susan Plummer, Vanessa, Samantha and Rachael, for the many trips to the walk-in fridge (in our garage!), the shuffling of equipment back and forth, slicing and dicing, the endless washing of dishes and sampling of dishes. We so appreciate all your help.

To all our farmers, ranchers, fishers, thank you for your tireless work. What you do is not easy, and most of the time under-recognized and under-appreciated. We want you to know we appreciate you. Remember, we cannot do anything without you. You are superheroes to us.

Thank you to all the extraordinary women we have worked for and with, and those we have gotten to know along the way in the business of food and drink: writers, chefs, bakers, winemakers, educators and makers of all kinds. You each create a better place for more women to find their space and a loud, clear voice.

INDEX